RICHELIEU

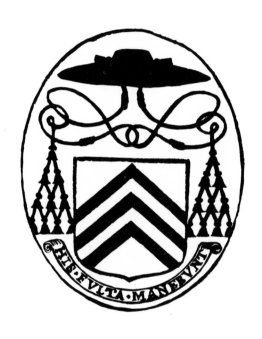

RICHELIEU

by Louis Auchincloss

A Studio Book

The Viking Press

New York

Panorama of Paris, approximately 1640. (*Photo Giraudon*)

First published in 1972 by The Viking Press, Inc. 625 Madison Avenue, New York, N.Y. 10022
Published simultaneously in Canada by The Macmillan Company of Canada Limited
SBN 670-59755-4. Library of Congress catalog card number: 72-81676. Printed in U.S.A.

For my old friend and former law associate, John R. Raben

Henri IV by Claudius Popelin. (Musée Condé, Chantilly. *Photo Giraudon*)

TABLE OF CONTENTS

Allegory: "Land where truth is born," showing Henri IV, Marie de Médicis, and the infant Louis XIII. French School, 17th century. (Musée des Beaux Arts, Amiens. *Photo Giraudon*)

Foreword

The golden glow that was setting over Europe in the first two decades of the seventeenth century is comparable to that of the first two decades of our own, except that it was not, like ours, the end of a long era of peace but the interregnum between two periods of carnage. The terrible religious strife of the sixteenth century had ended in England with Elizabeth, in France with Henri IV, and in the Netherlands with the truce with Spain. Even in the multitudinous and ever-feuding German states the Holy Roman Emperor Matthias showed sparks of tolerance. There seemed reason for men to catch their breath and to look about at a world where life might once again be worth living. Shakespeare in 1603, referring to the death of Elizabeth and to the accession of James I, saw nothing but good ahead:

> The mortal moon hath her eclipse endured,
> And the sad augurs mock their own presage;
> Incertainties now crown themselves assured,
> And peace proclaims olives of endless age.

Yet before a decade had run its course the playwright, in his final period of the romantic comedies, was showing signs of a philosophic but melancholy disillusionment. The last plays are bathed in a luminous sadness. A new world had been discovered across the seas; scientific inventions abounded; religious experiments in toleration had proved successful, but what did any of these things count against the irrationality of man? What did any amount of goodness avail a community when a Leontes could be jealous of a wife who manifestly

9

adored him, a marooned Sebastian ambitious for a kingdom that he could not even hope to reach, and a Cymbeline savagely contemptuous of a daughter who sought only to serve him? If men were determined to be unhappy—well, there were ways enough of achieving *that* goal. It seemed that the old spirit of Saint Bartholomew's Day was itching to ride again. Everybody wanted to get back to the business of killing.

The prevailing panic of the era was that the old, near-universal empire of Charles V, reassembled, would rise up to dominate a Europe restored to the ancient faith. To us today, brought up on Voltaire's quip that the Holy Roman Empire was neither holy nor Roman nor an empire, and educated to the concept of the Spanish monarchy as in somehow perpetual decline, it is difficult to believe that such a panic was reasonable. But we should consider how matters appeared to harassed Protestants at the beginning of the seventeenth century.

The empire of Charles V was split, it was true, but split among two Habsburg sovereigns related to each other over and over again by the incestuous practice of intermarriage in that family. The Holy Roman Emperor ruled tightly over Austria and Hungary and more loosely over all the German states. The Spanish king ruled, in addition to his own kingdom, Portugal, the Netherlands, Franche-Comté, Milan, the kingdom of the two Sicilies, and most of the New World. His domination of Italy, even to the papal states, was almost complete. What nations lay outside this vast Habsburg sphere of influence? France, torn by religious strife; England, not yet a great power of the continent; the untested Scandinavian countries; a divided Poland; and a semibarbaric Russia. If the Spanish monarch, enriched by all the gold of the New World, and the emperor, with his claim to leadership of all Christian sovereigns, worked together, who could withstand them? And just such cooperation their ministers constantly proclaimed.

Disaster for Europe began in 1610, when Henri IV of France was assassinated by a lunatic who deemed him insufficiently Catholic. In 1618 the Thirty Years' War started in Germany with Bohemia's defiance of the emperor. The rapid defeat of the Bohemian king in the Battle of the White Mountain by the emperor and the League of Catholic Princes made grimly clear to the German Protestant north that it would have to fight a long and costly conflict if it was not to be totally subdued by Emperor Ferdinand II, whose avowed goal was to eradicate the new faith. In 1621 the long truce between Spain and the Netherlands expired, and Philip III's minister Lerma went enthusiastically back to a savage, expensive, and fruitless war. The horror that settled over Europe was unequaled by anything since the fall of the Roman Empire, and the nightmare was intensified by a plague of superstition that caused the burning of a million witches.

France, at the beginning of the conflict, was paralyzed by internal divisions. Firstly, the southern regions were infested with an independent, well-organized Huguenot minority. This embattled sect held two hundred fortified towns in virtual independence of the French crown. La Rochelle on the west coast was almost a second capital to Paris, and the province of Languedoc in the southeast might have been a separate nation. Secondly, the great nobles operated in virtual independence of the crown, fortifying their domains, levying imposts, raising private armies, and carrying on private feuds. Finally, the king was a very young man dominated by a mother who was both pro-pope and pro-Spain. Had it not been for the appearance of a great first minister, France might have fallen into a division of autonomous provinces, an easy prey for the Habsburg cousins.

This was the situation when the cardinal de Richelieu began his second and final ministry in 1624. For eighteen years, until his death, he directed France with absolutely consistent internal and external policies. He first broke the power of the great nobles and of the Huguenots and united France under an absolute monarchy. After that, by diplomacy, by conspiracy, by bribes, by subsidies, and finally by outright war, he undermined and defeated his adversaries in Vienna and Madrid. Six years after his death, in 1648, the Treaty of Westphalia, which ended the Thirty Years' War, broke the Holy Roman Empire into a multitude of weak states. In 1659 the Treaty of the Pyrenees established the modern boundaries of France, which became the first power in Europe. Thenceforth it was to be a Bourbon, rather than a

Opposite: Philip IV of Spain, in hunting attire, by Velázquez. The pale face, like that of his cousin, opposite, reflects a self-confidence that excludes the least doubt that God made Habsburgs to rule the world. *Right:* Emperor Ferdinand II, in hunting attire, by Velázquez. Constant intermarriages preserved the Habsburg looks right into our own century. (The Prado Museum, Madrid. *Photos Anderson-Giraudon*)

Habsburg world. Richelieu believed at all times that he was accomplishing God's will, but he did not believe that God's will was necessarily expressed anywhere but in Paris, and not even in Paris, but in the Palais-Cardinal.

To accomplish his goal he used no new political or fiscal methods. To the philosophies of government and finance he contributed nothing. He simply picked up and employed the one tool that he found to hand: the power inherent in the French crown. The king was vested with an almost mystical authority, but it operated only when the subjects were literally within sight of their sovereign. What Richelieu did was to spread this authority throughout France so that royal representatives could act with the same power as their master. As one looks back today at the mess that faced him, it is hard to see what else he could have done. He had little interest in Catholic supremacy and no particular animus against the Huguenots. Once their military power had been broken, he was perfectly willing to accord them the right to worship as they pleased. In similar fashion, although an aristocrat himself and an admirer of the nobility, he did not hesitate to infuriate them by destroying the fortifications of their castles and stripping them of arms. The royal authority that he reinforced and re-created was to last, except for the disturbances that immediately followed his death, until the revolution in 1789. He was more than any one man the maker of modern France.

It is more difficult to assess his responsibility for the continuation of the terrible wars in Germany and Spain. Certainly millions died in these conflicts. It seems entirely possible to us today that the power of Spain and of the Holy Roman Empire might have declined anyway, without his interference. If this were so, he taxed the poor to the starvation point and sacrificed thousands of troops for nothing. Fortunately for him, he never knew such doubts. His conscience was appallingly clear.

One thing nobody can take from him. In an age of violent emotion, he was always dispassionate. In a time of muddy thinking, he was always clear. He saw the grandeur of the age of Louis XIV ahead of him and with it the triumph of French culture, and he pointed

LOVIS·XIV·DANS·SA·MINORITÉ

The young Louis XIV by Mignard. He was to preserve this pose for seven decades. One can foresee the
whole world of Versailles in the turn of his left foot. (Château de Champs. *Photo Lauros-Giraudon*)

a stern, constant finger toward these things. Whether he paid too much for them and what in the end they might be worth were not questions that concerned him. Law and order, as we should say today, were his obsessions: in government, in religion, in art, in literature. All Europe could go to rack and ruin so long as France was the ark of civilization. Anyone who wanted to be saved could get on board. It sometimes seems as if he tied the knots of his disciplines so tightly that our world is still engaged in undoing them.

"Birth of Louis XIII" by Peter Paul Rubens. Part of the series executed for Marie de Médicis'
Palais du Luxembourg, now in the Louvre. Hercules holds the infant prince. (*Photo Giraudon*)

Triple portrait of Richelieu by Philippe de Champaigne. (Reproduced by courtesy of the Trustees, The National Gallery, London)

I

The Bishop of Luçon

Armand Jean du Plessis, later cardinal-duc de Richelieu, was born, probably in Paris, on September 9, 1585, the third son of François, marquis de Richelieu, and his wife, Suzanne de La Porte, the daughter of a well-known member of the Paris bar and a councilor of the Parlement. Armand was thus the fruit of a union between the nobility and the upper bourgeoisie. It was frequently said that his father belonged to the minor nobility, but this was true only in the sense that he was not one of the great robber barons of France, like a Montmorency or a La Trémoille. François de Richelieu moved in the highest circles. He was a friend of Henri III, who made him Grand Provost of France and a knight of the Holy Ghost. It was François who with his own hands seized the mad monk who had assassinated his sovereign. But he was not too much of a Valois partisan to refuse to make his peace with Henri de Navarre, and he might well have become one of the great men of the new reign had he not been carried off by typhoid in 1590. François inherited the family melancholy and the family ambition. He had also a touch of the family madness. One of his uncles, Antoine, had been celebrated for his maniacal cruelty as an officer for the Catholic Guises in the religious wars.

The family had estates in Poitou to which the widowed Suzanne retired to raise her five children. If she had brought a fortune to the Richelieus, it must have been largely dissipated in maintaining a position at court, for she seems to have had constant trouble making ends meet. It was not so much that the Richelieus were poor as that they lacked the affluence to maintain the "state" which they deemed appropriate to their rank. The haughty old dowager marquise, a member of the great house of Rochechouart, who lived with them, probably constantly flung in her daughter-in-law's face the fact that her base blood was not balanced by any compensating infusion of wealth. The young Armand inherited his grandmother's prejudices, for all his life he labored to make the Richelieus one of the great families of France. One might say it was his hobby. No matter how much he was occupied with state duties he always had time to pick up a new farm or an abbey to swell his revenues or to add a new title to the list of those that he would ultimately distribute among his nephews. He never forgot the lean days of his Poitou childhood.

With care, Suzanne managed to look out for her three sons and two daughters. The eldest, Henri, had his role as marquis cut out for him. He would go to court. The second, Alphonse, was slated for the church to keep the revenues of the family-held bishopric of Luçon, on the Brittany border of Poitou, from going to a stranger. And Armand, despite his indifferent health, would go to Paris to be trained for the army. So far as we know he was perfectly amenable to this. He was called by a family title, the marquis de Chillou, and enrolled in the academy of Antoine de Pluvinel. He was never to regret his indoctrination in military matters.

Alphonse, however, changed the whole scheme. Already treading the borderline between mysticism and the insanity that was to characterize his later years, he suddenly announced to his family that he had decided to be a monk and not a bishop. He proved undissuadable, and Armand had to be removed from Monsieur de Pluvinel's courtly academy and sent to a seminary to study for the priesthood. The difference was less great in his century than it would have been today. In later years Richelieu would employ one cardinal-general against another: La Valette against the Infante Ferdinand of Spain. Military men were theologians, and priests wore armor.

After completing his studies Armand was still under the canonical age for ordination, and he set off to Rome to hasten the necessary dispensation. Many legends exist about his only visit to the papal capital. It was said that he dazzled the court of Paul V with his dialectical brilliance and feats of memory. He was reputed to have repeated an hour-long sermon, word for word, after hearing it once. The pope is supposed to have exclaimed with a laugh, after finding out that he had misrepresented the very age for which he was seeking a dispensation: "He will prove a great rascal!" But all we know for sure is that in 1607, at the age of twenty-two, he was ordained a priest and on the same day consecrated a bishop. When he returned to Paris and paid his respects to his father's old friend, Henri IV, the "green gallant" put an arm about his shoulders and called him affectionately "my bishop."

He did not, however, remain in court. Perhaps he wished the experience of organizing his own diocese. Perhaps he thought he was still too young and unconnected to get ahead in politics. Perhaps it was no longer practically possible to be an absentee bishop. The junior clergy were not as submissive as they once had been. But whatever the reason, his decision to immerse himself in his shabby bishop's palace in faraway Poitou was probably the right one. The knowledge that he gained of the church was vital to a statesman who was always going to be a priest as well.

His first concern was characteristic. It was with appearances. All his political life he was to insist that the trappings of power were an essential part of power itself. In 1609 we find him corresponding with a friend in Paris, one Madame de Bourges, about purchases for his palace and church:

> Madame:
> I received the copes [ecclesiastical mantles] that you sent. They came just when they were needed and are very handsome indeed and much appreciated by those for whom they were purchased. In my little barony I am now well enough liked by everybody— or so they would have me believe—but I need not tell you that things always *start* that way. I shall not lack occupation here, I assure you, for everything is in a state of such ruin that it will take a frightful lot of work to put it in order. I am very badly housed, and there is not a fireplace that does not smoke. You can judge from this that the last thing I needed was a cold winter, but there is no remedy except patience. I think I can promise you that I have the wretchedest bishopric in all of France, and the muddiest and most disagreeable, so I leave to

your imagination what must be the state of its Bishop! There is no place to take a walk, no garden, no avenue or anything like one, with the result that my house is really a prison. In closing, I must confess that we cannot find among the clothes you sent a tunic and a dalmatic of white taffeta which was to go with the white damask ornaments that you were having made for me. I think they must have been forgotten!

After the trappings comes the show of force, and we have more than a hint of the future disciplinarian of France in this epistle to an insubordinate vicar:

I deduce from your letter that you were in a bad mood when you picked up your pen. For my part, I am so fond of my friends that I wish only to see their good side. It might be wise of them to show me no other. Knowing how to control myself, thanks to God, I know how those beneath me should behave!

But he never lost sight, in the tumult of local affairs, of his real goal, which was always the court in Paris. A curious manuscript exists that he wrote in 1609 entitled: "Rules for my conduct at Court." It consists of a set of common-sense guides for the behavior of a young sycophant who wishes to get ahead in the court of Henri IV. They seem for the most part very obvious, even banal, and one wonders why a man who could repeat a whole sermon, word by word, as he was supposed to have done on the Roman visit, had to inscribe these precepts in order to remember them. Perhaps it was pride of authorship. Certainly, like many brilliant men, he had a weakness for a cliché. Take this example:

One must not show an inattentive spirit or a roving eye or a sad and melancholy visage when being addressed, but rather a graceful attention which is better manifested by silence than by any words or applause. The more honor one is shown, the humbler and more respectful one should be.

More pungent and sensible is this simple warning:

Remember to keep your mouth shut while the king is drinking!

A letter written three years later, in 1612, shows his continuing preoccupation with the affairs of the nation, particularly in diplomacy, and we pick up an early note of the jingoism that he was

HISPANIARVM ELISABET FRANCIÆ PRINCIPIS HISPANIARVM SPONSA D PHILIPPVS DE AVSTRIA PRINCEPS

Gallica se quantis attolet gloria rebus:
Bætica se quanto tellus Iactabit honore?
Connubio talli? foelix hymenœus, iberûm
Gallica pacifer qui lilia nectit oliuæ.

O France quelle palme? Espaigne o quel laurier
Vous doibt naistre du nœud de se saincte alliance
Trois foys heureux hymen, qui aux blancs lis de France
L'oliue porte-paix d'espaigne dois lier.

P   E

Preceding page: The future Philip IV of Spain with his bride, Elisabeth of France, sister of Louis XIII. Louis XIII was simultaneously married to Philip's sister, Anne of Austria. *Right:* The king's dinner, from the series of prints, *The Daily Occupations of Louis XIII*. The cardinal is seen behind the king's chair. (Bibliothèque Nationale, Paris. *Photos Bulloz*)

never to lose and that has been so extravagantly and traditionally praised by Gallic historians. He writes:

> The wise conduct and the affection and loyalty of good public servants will guarantee us from the evils within the kingdom. As for the evils without, I shall baptize them by a different name if they give us the opportunity to grow beyond our natural limits and to cover ourselves with glory at the expense of the enemies of France!

Sainte-Beuve, two centuries later, saw in this passage the instinctive cry of a soul filled with courage and virtue, a soul which was patriotic and French before anything else and which would always lose personal passions in the greatness of public events. Sainte-Beuve had not seen as much of the evils of rampant nationalism as we have today.

Richelieu's religious writings of this period would have little interest today but for his subsequent political career. It is worth noting, however, that his *Ordonnances Synodales* (1613) show a marked leniency for clandestine, as opposed to publicly scandalous, sins. Here is a sign of the statesman who would ultimately place the orderly society before all other civic values.

The assassination of Henri IV, who knew and liked him, was a great blow to Richelieu, but he transferred his attention to the widowed Marie de Médicis, now regent for the ten-year-old Louis XIII. He wrote her a long, unctuously flattering letter which he transmitted to his older brother, the marquis, who wisely declined to send it. Nobody has ever obtained a position of political importance by solicitation through the mails. The young bishop had to be cautioned to wait for a break. He waited four more years.

It came at last with the summoning of the Estates-General in 1614. This vast and colorful congregation of elected representatives from the three orders: nobles, clergy, and commons, was assembled to discuss—and to do nothing about—their various grievances. The commons resented the huge pensions paid by a weak queen-mother to guarantee (most ineffectively) the loyalty of the major peers; the latter resented the fact that the commons (heavily represented by lawyers) had made its parlement posts hereditary. Yet the nobles and commons were united in their opposition to the ultramontanism of the clergy who were inclined to set the pope over the crown. And all three orders had in common a solid loathing of the swaggering Italian adventurer Concini, who, by a marriage to Léonora Galigaï, a daughter of Marie de Médicis' old Florentine nurse, had climbed into royal favor. This infamous creature had actually been made a marshal of France and, although never a member of the Royal Council, he controlled the queen-mother, by sex or by flattery or by both, while amassing a fortune. He hoped to carve out an independent principality for himself before the king came of age.

The only thing that an ambitious young man could possibly hope to achieve in such an assembly was to be noticed, and Richelieu managed, with this in mind, to be elected a delegate. There was little that he could use for his own ends in the squabbles between the orders, but he was able at last to make something out of the hostility of his own clergy to Concini by taking the queen-mother's side and making a long address to the king and her before the entire assembly in one of the final sessions. Here he did not hesitate to extol the queen as the savior of France, and to advise her to take into her council more priests whose lack of family ties and earthly ambition would insure their loyalty and dedication to the crown. When one had only an hour to be heard, there was no room for subtlety.

Marie de Médicis remembered him. Others saw to this. The Capuchin monk, soldier-turned-priest, père Joseph (later to be known throughout Europe as the "Gray Eminence"), who already had noted the young bishop and who was an intimate of the royal household, pushed his cause. So did Claude Barbin, one of Concini's men, whom Richelieu had assiduously cultivated. When the court moved south for the double wedding of Louis XIII to Anne of Austria, daughter of Philip III of Spain, and of Louis' sister Elisabeth to the future Philip IV, Richelieu paid his respects to the queen-mother at Poitiers. He received the post of almoner to the new queen-consort, a girl of fifteen. It was a real start, for he now had a post at court and an excuse for constant attendance on Marie de Médicis.

Meeting of the Estates-General in 1614. (Bibliothèque Nationale, Paris. *Photo Giraudon*)

Above: The Spanish marriages: Philip of Spain to Elisabeth of France; Louis XIII to Anne of Austria. Marie de Médicis stands behind her son and daughter; Philip III of Spain behind his. (*Photo Larousse.*) *Right:* Marie de Médicis, in widow's attire, with the young Louis XIII. (Bibliothèque Nationale, Paris. *Photo Documentation Française*)

Above: Léonora Galigaï, wife of the maréchal d'Ancre. *Below:*
Christine de France, duchesse de Savoie, sister of Louis XIII.
Right: Celebration of the betrothal of Louis XIII and Anne of
Austria in the Place Royale (Place des Vosges), April 1612.
(Bibliothèque Nationale, Paris. *Photos Giraudon*)

The remarkable thing about Richelieu's early career was the speed of his advancement. It is a symptom either of the dearth of administrative talent surrounding the queen-mother or of the striking and immediately evident capacity of Richelieu that so many persons about her should have sought to give him a hand up. The flattery in which he had to engage has been viewed with scorn by some historians, but it was the accepted way for a young man to rise. In our own day a politician has to be tactful, diplomatic, amusing, and complimentary with the crowds that he may be lucky enough to address. Nobody bothered with crowds in the seventeenth century because they had no votes. A foolish woman was the repository of all political power in Paris. If one wanted to get ahead, it was through her, and that was simply that. The price of political power lay in writing this kind of letter to the queen-mother:

> I dedicate myself to your service, entreating God to increase my years only to increase yours and (without depriving me of His grace) to overwhelm me with disasters in order to overwhelm Your Majesty with prosperity.

Or this to the prince de Condé:

> My zeal in your service will never allow me to yield to any other the title that I shall fervently guard for the end of my days: that of your most humble servant.

This last seems peculiarly hypocritical as Richelieu at the time was probably planning to put his correspondent in jail. Henri II de Bourbon, prince de Condé, grandson of a paternal uncle of Henri IV, was next in line to the throne after Louis XIII's brother Gaston and had been told by a soothsayer that he would be king of France at thirty-five. He was in a constant state of armed rebellion against the queen-mother, and it seems likely that it was Richelieu who gave her the characteristically bold advice to arrest him and lock him up in the Bastille. Marie, trembling, brought herself at last to issue the necessary order. She expected the skies to fall, but nothing happened. Condé's old mother drove about Paris in her carriage, shrilly calling the people in the streets to arms, but they only gaped at her. It was a striking

Celle je suis qui fais regner les Roys   Et maintenir la Paix et la Milice
Qui scay regir les Armes et les Loix   En corrigeant des hommes la malice.

fournier pinx.
Thomas de Leu fecit

Marie de Médicis, enthroned as regent of France, armed with a sword and the scales of justice.

example of the power of the crown when the crown only chose to use it.

Condé was arrested on September 1, 1616. On November 25 Richelieu entered the Council as one of the secretaries of state. In a matter of weeks he was the acting first minister. As Disraeli would have put it, he had climbed to the top of the greasy pole. But he was to come right down again.

Henri II de Bourbon, prince de Condé, first prince of the blood. Although only a second cousin of Louis XIII, he was, for the first twenty-eight years of the latter's reign, second in line to the throne.

II

Brief Power

Marie de Médicis was descended from bankers and Habsburgs, and she was as extravagant as she was proud. Her father was Grand Duke Francis of Florence, and her mother the archduchess Johanna of Austria, daughter of Emperor Ferdinand I. It was the latter connection that Marie never forgot. Johanna had introduced Habsburg rigor and Habsburg gloom into the cheerful Italian court, but she had died when Marie was only three. The grand duke then married the notorious Bianca Capello, and Marie and her sister were brought up away from court. Her uncle Ferdinand succeeded her father, as there was no female succession under Florentine law, and Marie had to wait until she was twenty-seven—very much an old maid in those days—before he found her a husband. But then he made up for it. He used her great fortune to buy her the greatest sovereign in Europe.

She did not appreciate the "green gallant." But then she never appreciated anything really first-rate. She could see nothing in Henri IV but his infidelity and nothing in France but a source of gifts to her favorites. One sees in Rubens' many versions of her fat, powdered, pale face with its pouting eyes, a hopelessly difficult woman. She wanted power, but she was lazy and ignorant. She wanted love, but she was heartless. She wanted parties and gaiety, but she had no true vivacity or sense of humor. She may have seemed rather attractively majestic at a first meeting, with her ready responsiveness, her loud laugh, her stately affability, her imposing presence, and massive jewels, but soon enough, no doubt, her basic vulgarity and egotism came out. She was shrill without being domineering, aggressive without being strong,

Marie de Médicis by Rubens. No other likeness captures so brilliantly her force, egotism, and stupidity. (Musée du Louvre, Paris. *Photo Giraudon*)

shrewd without being imaginative, bigoted without being religious. Yet, what could Europe have expected of these women who were sent off, totally unprepared, to foreign courts and mated to sovereigns for whom they had not the smallest inclination? Marie de Médicis had been prepared by nobody for the absolute power that she now greedily grasped.

She was to stretch her influence as far as she could. Ultimately she was to be mother, not only of the king of France, but of the queens of Spain and England and of the duchess of Savoy. It was a dazzling social position for Europe in the seventeenth century, but a social position is as strong as its base. Marie lost hers when she exiled herself from France in 1631. Her sons-in-law in Madrid and London could not abide her, and she died ten years later, an international drifter, in the court of the elector of Cologne.

But in 1616 everything was still going her way. The king was of age—he was fifteen—but he had urged his mother to continue to handle the government. It was generally believed that this sullen, morose, unattractive boy, totally dedicated to hunting, could be led by the nose. Marie seemed to be in power indefinitely, and as Louis enjoyed poor health and showed no interest in his young bride, the future seemed to belong to Gaston, her younger son and favorite, known as "Monsieur," a youth possessed of good looks, smooth manners, and great charm. But if Marie and Gaston prospered, nobody else did.

The prince de Condé was in the Bastille, where he was to remain for another two years, but this was the only favorable factor in the domestic and foreign scene that faced Richelieu as the new senior member of the Council. France was weak abroad and weak at home. The treasury had been depleted by Marie's inroads to satisfy the great nobles. And, worse still, the power that Richelieu required so desperately to put things in order was far from assured. He had some control over the queen-mother, but she was a wilful creature and devoted to the abominable Concini, who strutted about the Louvre, followed by dozens of gentlemen in attendance, a blatant, gorgeously bedizened figure who put the young king in the shadows. Concini was more intent on building up his fortune than he was in controlling France's destiny, but he still had to be consulted in matters of state if only because of his vanity. Moreover, Marie was basically opposed to the strong national position that Richelieu already wished to take. She was always pro-Rome and pro-Spanish, more Habsburg than Bourbon, more Habsburg even than Médici. So completely was the bishop of Luçon identified with her interests that the first reports of the Spanish ambassador to his home office were actually that he was a friend of Spain!

What was Richelieu's hold over the queen-mother? Was he her lover? It seems unlikely. His name has never been reliably associated with that of any woman, and he hardly seems to have been the type to appeal to Marie—judging at least from her inclination for Concini. It seems more probable that he held her as he later held her son: by his extraordinary ability to get her the things she wanted. But if he was to be an independent statesman—as he most certainly intended—an ultimate rupture was unavoidable. His first ministry was simply not long enough to bring it about.

In his few months of power he accomplished little, but he showed at least that he was aware of the problems. A struggle between Venice and Savoy on one side and both Habsburg powers on the other had been complicated by the totally unauthorized expedition of the Protestant governor of Dauphiné across the border into Piedmont to protect the duke of Savoy from Spain. Richelieu at once showed his ability to use a *fait accompli* to his own advantage. Instead of repudiating the French invasion he seized upon it as a chance to bargain from a position of strength and made a desperate, if unsuccessful effort to negotiate a general settlement. He did not have time, as things turned out, to bring it about, but he was able to impress observers. Nobody who dealt even briefly with Richelieu ever forgot him.

Richelieu must have almost at once become aware that he had come to power by the wrong ladder. The young king was not, after all, a cipher. He was brooding; he was biding his time. And he loathed Concini and all those associated with him. There is evidence that Richelieu was in correspondence with Charles d'Albert, later duc de Luynes, the king's falconer, a handsome Provençal, who had been quietly building a secure dominance over the shy boy sovereign who was dazzled by his companion's brawn and athleticism. Too late. Why should Luynes share the royal favor for which he had astutely labored? Let the bishop of Luçon enjoy the good graces of the king's harridan of a mother and of her vulgar braggadocio of a lover! Richelieu must have been sick at heart as he saw himself identified with the pack of riffraff about Concini, hated by all the court and doomed. Was this the end of all his schemes? Was it the end of France?

He was lucky to escape with his life. Louis, spurred on by Luynes, finally acted, and Concini was shot down like a mad dog as he was entering the Louvre, ostensibly for resisting arrest. His little empire did not survive him by five minutes. Even Marie de Médicis turned on his widow and snapped at those who asked how they could possibly tell the poor woman of her husband's death: "If you can't tell it to her, sing it to her!" The remark is the epitome of the woman's callousness and vulgarity. The body of Concini was torn to bits by an angry mob, and the bishop of Luçon narrowly escaped the same fate when his carriage passed the scene. By leading the crowd in a cheer for the king, he was allowed to pass.

He took his medicine well. He followed the queen-mother to her exile at Blois and continued to serve her. But this was not far enough for the jealous, suspicious, and now all-powerful Luynes. Richelieu was exiled to Avignon, then a papal conclave surrounded by French territory, where he remained for two quiet years writing the religious treatises, *Principal Points of the Faith of the Catholic Church* and *Instruction of a Christian.* He also maintained a lengthy correspondence with old friends at both courts, the king's and the queen-mother's, particularly with père Joseph, who kept him from fading from Marie's easily forgetting mind.

In 1619 the queen-mother escaped from her gilded prison at Blois and placed herself in armed revolt. Luynes knew that he needed Richelieu to control her and recalled him from Avignon. Richelieu went straight to the queen-mother, took over control of her affairs, and at once opened negotiations for peace. He saw his way clearly enough now. Only through Marie could he come back to power. Marie and Louis

Above: Charles d'Albert (or Alberti), duc de Luynes. (*Photo Jean Roubier-Larousse*). *Below:* The Bastille in the 17th century, where royal prisoners were allowed to dwell in some comfort, with their own servants and plates, but dismally. (Bibliothèque Nationale, Paris. *Photo Larousse*)

Pendant que le beau monde au long de ces murailles,
Fait valoir son credit a la faueur du cours.

De pauures malheureux resuent leurs funerailles,
Dans le triste seiour de ces obscures Tours.

Left: Nicolas de l'Hôpital, marquis de Vitry, the captain of the royal bodyguard. He was in charge of the murder of d'Ancre, and was rewarded with a marshal's baton. *Below:* The terrible scenes of the murder of d'Ancre and the mutilation of his body. Some of these events were witnessed by Richelieu, who learned the fate of fallen ministers. *Opposite:* Concino Concini, maréchal d'Ancre. (Musée du Louvre, Paris. *Photo Giraudon*)

LE MARESCHAL DANCRE 1624

Louis XIII as a boy. (The Uffizi Gallery, Florence. *Photo Alinari-Giraudon*)

had to be reunited, and there had to be no more Concinis. It might have seemed to some that he was betraying his mistress by settling her revolt, even on advantageous terms to her, more as the king's agent than as hers, but this gave him no trouble. It was always characteristic of Richelieu to take the larger view. Marie had no future as a rebel; her place was with her son. Everybody's first duty was to the king. One sees already the commanding logic of his thinking, like a great, straight highway through the heart of France.

Luynes promised to obtain a cardinal's hat for him and then wrote privately to Rome to defer it. But Richelieu could afford to wait. The favorite's star was waning. Luynes was glad enough to marry his nephew to Richelieu's niece. Louis was already disillusioned with him. When Luynes died of a fever after failing to capture Montauban, a Protestant stronghold in the south, there was a general feeling that the king would have to recall Richelieu to the Council. He was the only man who seemed able to make order out of the shambles into which government had fallen.

Louis, however, remembered Concini; he refused to give in. It was two and a half years before he could overcome his aversion to his mother's bishop. When on August 13, 1624, Richelieu at last received the royal summons to resume his seat in the Council it was seven years since his dismissal. The five months of his first ministry had been paid for with eighty-seven of watchful waiting.

But things were different now. He had finally received his cardinal's hat, and he used his princely rank to take precedence over others in the Council. He was not given the official title of first minister for another five years, but, practically speaking, he occupied that office from the beginning. Also, the king was no longer a boy; he was a man of twenty-three. Marie de Médicis still had considerable influence on him and still occupied a place on the Council, but her power and prestige were nothing to what they had been in 1616. If Louis' health and grudging good will only lasted, there was a chance for Richelieu to accomplish his task. In fact they were to last until the latter's death.

Ecstasy of Richelieu. He is shown in communion with the spirit of monarchical France. (Bibliothèque Nationale, Paris. *Photo Larousse*)

Louis XIII, shown allegorically with his two kingdoms, France and
Navarre, by Simon Vouet. (Musée du Louvre, Paris. *Photo Giraudon*)

III

The King and the Cardinal

The relationship between Louis XIII and Richelieu remains a fascinating mystery. Some historians have claimed that the king bitterly resented the domination of the older, abler man, that he tolerated him only for his indispensable talents, that he was disgusted by his ulcers and bored by his shop talk. Others have argued that Louis was a creature of no character or will power, mere putty in the cardinal's hands. Still others have insisted that he was a great monarch and an exacting taskmaster who appreciated Richelieu's abilities and employed him as the right man for the job, but who subjected all his decisions to a scrutinizing and critical review. And, finally, there are those who maintain that the two men were devoted to each other and worked in close and happy communion for the welfare of France. There is probably some truth in each of these theories.

It must be remembered that the partnership lasted for eighteen years during all of which the sovereign and his minister had to be a great deal together or at least in constant communication. In any such long, necessarily intimate business relationship, every kind of feeling is bound to crop up, particularly in the boss. Louis XIII undoubtedly appreciated the cardinal's efficiency and was probably glad to have such a strong hand at his elbow, but he would not have been human had he not been subject to fits of violent jealousy and resentment. He must have known that the courts of Europe regarded Richelieu as the real master. And then Louis was very much an outdoors man, a passionate hunter, while the cardinal's idea of enjoying fresh air was to sit in a formal garden and sniff flowers. Yet for all their intellectual and physical incompatibility, their correspondence shows unmistakable signs of genuine mutual affection. We know in the age of Freud that there is nothing impossible about a love-hate relationship.

Louis had had a lonely, unhappy childhood. The great, dazzling father had been slaughtered when Louis was only ten, and he had had to depend thereafter on a preoccupied mother who succeeded in being both cold and violent. Had King Henri lived, his famous charm and warmth might have made a different man of Louis, but dead he simply represented the ideal of the warrior and sovereign that his son could never achieve. Marie de Médicis not only neglected the child; she over-disciplined him. Louis was frequently birched. He grew up a stammering, morose, resentful boy. Small wonder that the handsome, older, athletic Luynes, with a small show of affection, should have become his god.

The little kingdom that he and Louis created out of falconry might have been the model of the greater state which they had not yet effectively brought under their control. It had its own ministers, officers, subjects, and finances. The birds were divided into two categories: (1) the birds of the chamber, being the trained, captive falcons, a whole plumed court, and (2) the wild birds, consisting of one hundred forty different species that Louis liked to hunt. All the birds, trained or wild, were under the jurisdiction of the grand falconer of France, and his feudal subordinates were ranked under the different categories of flight, such as "flight in the field" or "flight by the river." These flights were in turn broken down into the different species of birds, and each species was assigned its particular number of falcons, greyhounds, and men. To the heron, for example, were assigned fifteen men, four greyhounds, and twelve falcons. Luynes himself and ten men were assigned to the kites; his brother to the crows and merlins.

It should have been obvious, to the alert, that behind all this trivia was the mind of an administrator or at least of a would-be administrator. The one thing that Louis seems never to have forgotten for a minute was that he was king. He might be of poor health (he became tubercular early); he might be sluggish of wit; he might stammer; he might suffer from fits of rage and depression; he might cut a poor figure with the ladies compared to the strutting peacocks of his court—but what did any of that matter in the glare of the overwhelming truth of his sovereignty? Consider how many dim souls through the ages have comforted themselves for their inferiority with fantasies of power. With Louis the fantasy was true! It is easy to see that he could build a life on it.

He began to develop a sense of the inviolability of his kingship at an early age. Nobody but Luynes—not even Richelieu—had the least suspicion of it until Concini was shot down in the Louvre. What a heady moment that must have been for the brooding boy, to see blasted before his eyes the loathed usurper of his prerogatives, the vulgar foreigner who had dared to condescend to him, the possible occupant of his brassy mother's bed! Only some fifteen years after Shakespeare wrote *Hamlet*, this similar drama was enacted across the Channel. Richelieu, identified with the butchered monster in Louis' mind, was lucky not to share his fate. It was a setback from which only a man of the greatest astuteness could ever have recovered.

Life now began to develop according to Louis' plan. When he went into the field against rebellious nobles, rebellion melted away before the royal standard. His belief in himself was shared by millions. The right of kings *was* divine! A strong royal rule was the answer not only to the problems of France; it was the answer to the problems of Louis. It dignified every personal failure. For example, was it shyness and timidity or even fear, that inhibited him from sexual intercourse? Certainly not! It was royal virtue. When Luynes suggested that a command would easily overcome the scruples of a court virgin, he exposed himself to this stinging rebuke: "The more I am king and in a position to make myself prevail, the more it behooves me to remember what God forbids. I shall pardon your imprudence this time. Let it not be repeated." What a splendid way to be able to pass off the dread of impotence!

Like so many persons of weak nature, Louis fortified himself by inflicting punishment. He was quite merciless with respect to pardons, even where beautiful wives of high rank flung themselves on their knees in his path. Unlike Richelieu, who was merciless out of policy alone, Louis had a sadistic streak. It was said that at the siege of Montauban he had fatally wounded Huguenots put in the dried-out ditches surrounding the château where he was quartered and mimicked the contortions of the dying. It was permissible, according to his dim lights, to enjoy the sufferings of others if they merited their fate. Playing a game of checkers at the time that his former favorite, Cinq-Mars, was led to the block, he glanced at his watch and commented: "I should like to see what kind of a face Monsieur le Grand is making now." When told that all France was pleading for Montmorency's life, he said coldly: "I should not be the king if I had the feelings of private persons." The cardinal, on the other hand, was not titillated by suffering—and was less concerned with justice. The block was a place of business, no more. He wrote in his memoirs: "In the course of ordinary affairs, justice requires authentic proof. It is not necessarily so in matters of state. There, occasions arise where one must start with an execution."

But unfurling the royal standard and ordering executions were not alone going to unify France under the royal will. The power was there in the crown, but that power had to be exercised, and to do that Louis, who was young and inexperienced and lazy, needed a minister. He found himself surrounded by incompetents. His mother was ignorant and mulish; Luynes had no vision; Sully was too old; the great nobles cared for nothing but their own self-aggrandizement. Absolute power was not much fun when one never had a clear view of what was going on. And the one thing on which everybody, friend or enemy of Richelieu, seemed to agree was that he had a clear view.

In eighteen years, despite many ugly differences, Louis never once demoted his first minister. But he thought about it at times, and, much worse, he listened to people who suggested it. This was one of the ways in which he most bedeviled Richelieu. Without ever overtly supporting a plot against the cardinal—and why should he have plotted against a man whom he could summarily dismiss?—he nonetheless gave the occasional impression that he would not be unhappy to see him done away with. When Cinq-Mars hinted that Richelieu was, after all, only mortal, the king replied that one could be damned for killing a priest. Obviously a rash young hothead was going to deduce from this that the king would welcome the deed if his own conscience was clear. The illusion that Louis was psychologically the cardinal's slave, yearning to be freed, led many men to the scaffold. They would find the weak sovereign turned into an implacable judge.

Why did he do it? Why did he increase the tension under which his tension-wracked minister was always suffering? Partly, perhaps, from his streak of sadism, the same that had made him, in the days of Luynes' favoritism, confront the latter with evidence of his young wife's infidelity. But it seems more likely that it was a mortification with his own lesser abilities that required the retention of Richelieu's greater ones. It was necessary to Louis' ego, as we have seen, that he should be a great monarch. It was the only way, to put matters basically, that he could be a man. And he could be a great monarch only with Richelieu at the helm. He had the sense and vision to grasp this central fact, but he did not have the temperament to accept it gracefully—at least not at all times. He had a nasty temper, and when he was in a mood to show "my cousin" (as kings addressed cardinals) who was boss, he promptly did so.

Richelieu had underestimated the young king during his first ministry in 1616. He never did so again. Every waking hour he recognized that the source of his authority was in this moody, jealous, unpredictable man. When Richelieu was not with him—and it was better for them to be frequently apart—he had his silent representatives constantly in the royal presence. Olivares in Spain adopted the same policy with Philip IV, although the Spanish king was much more subject to personal domination than Louis XIII. No matter how late Olivares had toiled the night before, it was always he, early up and in full court dress, who parted the curtains of the monarch's bed and bade him good morning.

It is important, however, to understand that jealousy on one hand and apprehension on the other were only a part of this tangled relationship. The partnership of shared power, a partnership that separated them from all the governed, inevitably drew them together at their lonely altitude. The possession of state secrets acted as a glue.

53

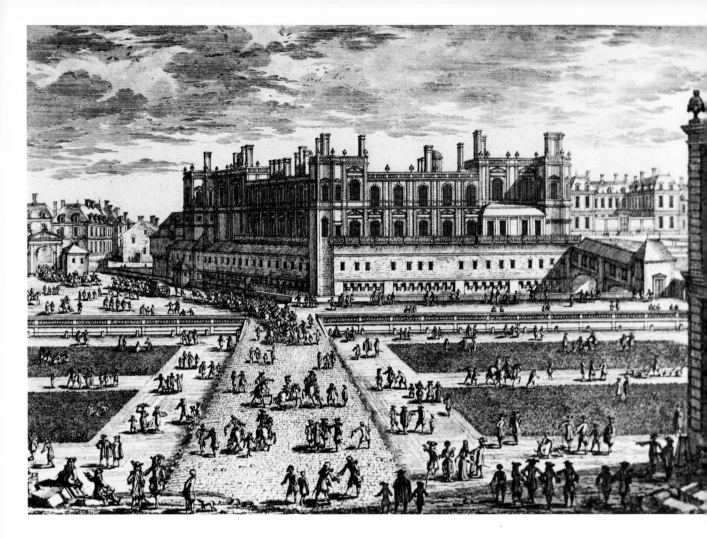

Above: Château de Saint-Germain, preferred residence of Louis XIII. Richelieu's own château at Rueil was conveniently close by. *Left:* Louise de La Fayette, lady-in-waiting to Anne of Austria. Her brother was an ancestor of the American revolutionary hero. (Bibliothèque Nationale, Paris. *Photo Larousse*). *Opposite:* Marie de Hautefort challenges Louis XIII to recapture a letter that she has concealed in her bodice.

From the series, *The Daily Occupations of Louis XIII:* "The Morning Promenade." (Bibliothèque Nationale, Paris. *Photo Bulloz*)

That Richelieu and the king knew who was corresponding with Spain, that they even knew treasonable facts about Queen Anne and her circle, must have been the occasion, in court gatherings, for more than one ironical glance exchanged between them. And then, too, there had to be times when Louis' recognition of the success of his servant's policies inspired a genuine admiration, from which something like affection might easily have grown. In the great moments of joint victory, when they rode together into a prostrate La Rochelle, or entered Savoy through the Suse pass, or read dispatches of the fall of Breisach, their joint elation may have flared into something like friendship.

For those who maintain that the king consistently detested Richelieu, the tone of their correspondence poses a difficult question. Richelieu's earnest protestations of humble devotion can, of course, be dismissed as the conventional hypocrisy of the day, but how is one to account for the affection constantly expressed by the monarch? No tradition or convention dictated this. When Louis quit the siege of La Rochelle, sick and bored, leaving Richelieu behind to do the dirty work, he sent this dispatch from the first stop:

> I could hardly say a word when I left you. I was too upset. You must learn to have confidence in my devotion and believe that I will keep my promises—yes, till death! When I think that you are no longer with me, I feel lost!

There was a similar correspondence at the siege of Corbie when the situation was reversed, and it was Louis who was going to the army, leaving the sick cardinal in Paris. Richelieu tried to dissuade the king from going. The latter lost his temper, and Richelieu backed down. Immediately Louis suffered remorse. Le Bouthillier, the cardinal's envoy, hurriedly wrote to Richelieu: "The king imagines that you are angry. For God's sake, if you have written anything to give him that idea, tell me, and I'll hold back the letter!" At the same time Louis wrote to his "cousin": "I am in despair over the heedlessness with which I wrote to you yesterday concerning my journey. I beg of you, burn the letter and forget what it contained. Believe that I never meant to anger you, and that I am always willing unconditionally to follow your good advice."

Even more indicative of affection on the king's part than the

Facsimile of Louis XIII's famous letter to Richelieu at La Rochelle. "My cousin: I am told you are resolved to join the battle at sea. For God's sake change your mind and don't expose yourself. I want you to take the same care of yourself that you would if you were I myself. . . ."

Mon Cousin on ma dit aujourd'huy,
que vous aurez pris resolution de
vous anbarquer sur un vesseau pour
estre au conbat, je vous conjure
au nom de Dieu de changer la resolution que
vous auez prise, et de ne vous
mettre point en lieu ou vous puisiés
courre aucune fortune, je vous en
prie encornes unefois dene vous mettre
en lieu ou vous puisiés courre, je
tiendray le mesme soin que vous,
aures de vous comme si cettoit de moy
mesme que vous lussies, cert le plus
grand temoygnage daffection que vous
me puisiés temoygner que danoir soin de vous

letters of professed warmth are the large number of those, written in his own hand, that kept the cardinal up to date on day-to-day occurrences. Louis would dash these off at Saint-Germain from where a courier would presumably gallop off to deliver them to Rueil or to the Palais-Cardinal. Sometimes the king would write more than once on the same day. Here, for example, is one of two letters written from Saint-Germain on October 10, 1641, after word had come through of the death of the cardinal-infante, Queen Anne's brother, then a Spanish general operating against France on the Belgian frontier:

> The queen learned at noon from her ladies of the death of the cardinal-infante. She went to bed and wept a bit. I went to her immediately, and we laughed together—about other matters. I can assure you that this affliction will not make her lose her appetite and that she will not eat a mouthful less. I bid you good night—Louis.

The tone is casual, intimate, jocose. The two men know that the death of an able Spanish general is not to be regretted and that the queen, after all, has not seen him since childhood . . . still, a brother is a brother. The thing to note about the letter is the habit of dependency that it shows. When anything happened, the king's first thought was: What will Richelieu say?

The cardinal had also to deal with the fact that Louis was homosexual. This might have been easier to cope with had Louis faced it himself, but he did not. His was a classic case: the early death of a great, strong, adulated father, the hero of a hundred love affairs, and the survival of a possessive, dominating, unloving mother. We see Louis seeking all the outward marks of masculinity: in the hunting field, on the battlefield, in the bawdry-talking barracks—everywhere but in my lady's chamber. When the time came for his marriage to be consummated, Luynes had to carry him, kicking and struggling, to Anne's bed. It is hardly surprising, under the circumstances, that twenty more years were required to produce Louis XIV. The wonder is that he was ever produced at all.

Louis was attracted to two women, both ladies of the queen's household, Mademoiselle de Hautefort and Mademoiselle de La Fayette, but in each case the relationship remained strictly chaste. Mademoiselle de Hautefort was a bold, teasing beauty who mocked Louis for his reluctance to touch her and hid a letter that he asked to see in her bosom, challenging him, if he wanted it, to reach in and take it. He did not avail himself of the privilege, nor did her favor last long. Mademoiselle de La Fayette was much more to his taste. Her terror of losing her virginity was delightfully flattering to a lover who had no intention of taking it. Louis' ardor increased to fever pitch with the sense of his virtue in not seizing fruit that was so gratifyingly forbidden. When Mademoiselle de La Fayette took the veil, he went to her convent in Paris and had long talks with her through the grille. The compliant mother superior assured Majesty that an exception could be made in his case which would allow him to see her alone in the parlor, but Louis shook his head, scandalized. A good monarch should ask no favors that a subject could not have!

With the boys it was different. There can be little question that he was in love with Cinq-Mars in a way that he never was with the two ladies. Tallemant des Réaux says that he could not keep his hands off the beautiful young soldier and that they would go to bed together naked in the afternoon, but Tallemant was a fearful gossip, and, besides, he was writing a generation later. Still, the violence of Louis' passion and the rudeness that he tolerated in his petulant young friend—a most unusual feature of this affair—suggest that the course of love with Cinq-Mars was less than platonic. It may seem naïve in our times even to question this, but it must be remembered that the king was so carefully watched that any lack of evidence of sexual activity may always have meant the lack of such activity. There is no sure proof that Louis went to bed with his favorites, though there is considerable evidence that he wanted to.

He liked to recruit strapping young men as his musketeers. In a postscript to a letter to Saint-Simon, then on a military expedition to Lorraine, the king writes:

> They tell me there's a sergeant in Picardie called Rostaine who has quite a reputation. If he's as fine a looking fellow as they say, tell his captain to send him to me.

Henri d'Effiat, marquis de Cinq-Mars. (*Photo Larousse*)

Richelieu probably felt about the king's homosexuality the way he felt about Protestantism: that it was an unattractive taste not to be worried about so long as it did not get out of hand and threaten the sacred unity of France. If his master wanted boy friends, he had no objection so long as he, Richelieu, could pick them, to be sure that they would be nonpolitical. The trouble was that one could never be certain. It was Richelieu himself, after all, who introduced Cinq-Mars to the king.

The cardinal, for all his nervousness, for all his sensitivity and emotionalism, was essentially a very masculine man. Louis, on the other hand, for all his hunting and crudeness and barrack stories, for all his military swagger, had a feminine personality. He even danced in one of his own ballets in female garb. Although it is hardly likely that Louis would have been physically attracted to a minister who was older and sickly, the latter, as a strong, domineering male figure, swathed in priestly robes, may have suggested a double parental image, father and mother, a sort of beneficent surrogate. Certainly there is a little-boy quality in the lovelorn Louis' appeal to the cardinal to act as umpire in his disputes with Cinq-Mars.

Louis could not have altogether hated the man whom he thus brought into intimate contact with his lovers' quarrels. It is a curious picture: the arbiter of Europe's destinies sitting gravely over the spats between his master and this brash, dissolute, impossible but charming young man. Louis and Cinq-Mars used to sign formal contracts to regulate their behavior to each other. Here is a sample:

> November 26, 1639. The undersigned hereby certify that they are perfectly contented and satisfied with each other as of this date and resolve to continue their excellent understanding in the future. In witness whereof they have subscribed this document: Louis. Effiat de Cinq-Mars.

And here is one, five months later, on May 9, 1640. As master of the king's horse, Cinq-Mars was addressed in court as "Monsieur le Grand."

> His Majesty has seen fit to promise Monsieur le Grand that he will undertake not to lose his temper with him throughout this campaign and that if Monsieur le Grand should give him cause

to do so, His Majesty will simply place the matter before Monsieur le Cardinal so that he may advise Monsieur le Grand how to correct any conduct that may have displeased the king. This mutual understanding has been entered into by the king and Monsieur le Grand in the presence of His Eminence. Signed: Louis. Effiat de Cinq-Mars.

A good picture of how the king and the cardinal worked together is given in the memoirs of the maréchal de Bassompierre. Bassompierre, a great gallant of the court, a younger favorite of Henri IV, a first-rate soldier, and a famous lover, had been betrothed as a young man to the beautiful heiress Charlotte de Montmorency, but the engagement in that day of rigorous forms had been broken off because of his failure to call on one of her aunts. Brokenhearted, he had had to witness her marriage to the prince de Condé, whom his master, old King Henri, now infatuated with the girl himself, hoped would prove a *mari complaisant*. Condé, however, took his young bride abroad to guard her from the royal attentions, and Bassompierre distracted himself with wars and other loves. His memoirs are cluttered with military operations, but there are some vivid glimpses of Louis XIII and the minister into whose bad graces poor Bassompierre ultimately fell. Here is one that illustrates the constant assiduousness with which the cardinal had to study his master's moods.

In 1629, when the king, the cardinal, and Bassompierre were with the army at Suse in north Italy to raise the siege of Casale, the Genoese ambassador requested a formal audience with the king, but sent word privately to Bassompierre through the papal nuncio, asking him to take up with His Majesty the question of whether or not, representing a sovereign republic, he could remain covered in the royal presence. It was a tricky point because France had certain claims on Genoa that such a concession might appear to invalidate. Still, it was diplomatically advisable to give in. The nuncio explained to Bassompierre that he had already discussed the matter with the cardinal and that the latter had suggested that Bassompierre was just the man to approach the king, who, always jealous of his royal prerogative, might be expected to resist the Genoese claim. It was Richelieu's game, of course, to thrust an unpopular message on another's shoulders. Bassompierre, no fool, went straight to the cardinal, and the two discussed the matter frankly. It was finally agreed that Bassompierre should broach the matter to the king, and that Richelieu and the other marshals should back him up. After dinner at the Council Bassompierre carried out his part of the bargain, and the king, as anticipated, promptly lost his temper. The cardinal said soothingly:

> If you please, Sire, may I suggest that you ask the advice of the gentlemen present and then judge the matter as you see best?

The king then turned in surly fashion to Bassompierre and snapped:

> I'll start with you. However, I already know your opinion, and I certainly won't follow it. You think the Genoese should be covered because Don Augustin Fiesque thinks so, and he's one of your cronies.

Bassompierre, irritated, replied:

> Sire, if it will please you to reflect on my past actions you will recognize that the good of your service and your own greater glory have always been my principal interest. I have nothing to do with the Republic of Genoa, and even if I did, my interest there would always bow to yours. Don Augustin Fiesque is my friend, it is true, but he owes me a good deal more than I owe him, and even if it were the other way around, you must think me very light and inconsiderate if you imagine I would deceive you to oblige him. The oath which I took at your Council obligates me to give you my best advice according to my conscience, but since you judge so ill of me I abstain.

The king then became furious.

> You are on my Council and draw my wages. I command you to give me your advice!

Here the cardinal whispered to Bassompierre:

> For God's sake, tell him and stop arguing.

Bassompierre then had the temerity to make fun of the king:

Since Your Majesty insists upon my opinion, here it is. I have no doubt whatever that your rights and those of the crown you wear will perish utterly if you grant the Genoese what they are asking.

The king rose in fury and said that Bassompierre would soon find out who was the master. Here the cardinal intervened to calm him down. His little plan would now work out. Louis was always more tractable after an explosion of temper. He would soon be bored with the subject. And, indeed, when the Genoese ambassador appeared in the royal presence, he had his hat on.

François, maréchal de Bassompierre.

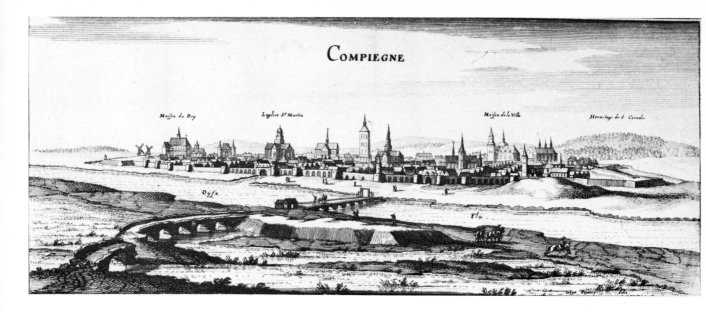

COMPIEGNE

Maison du Roy   L'eglise St Martin   Maison de la Ville   Hermitage de S. Cornelis

Oyse   Fla

ANNE D'AVSTRICHE. III. du Non. Royne de France & de Nauare

Above: Compiègne and the royal château. *Left:* Anne of Austria. (*Photo Bulloz*)

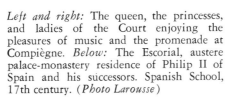

Left and right: The queen, the princesses, and ladies of the Court enjoying the pleasures of music and the promenade at Compiègne. *Below:* The Escorial, austere palace-monastery residence of Philip II of Spain and his successors. Spanish School, 17th century. (*Photo Larousse*)

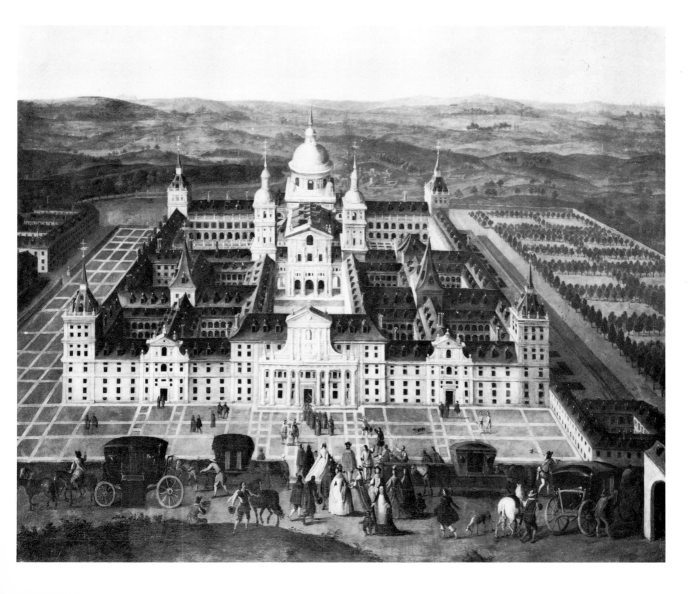

Above: Instruction for the duel. (Bibliothèque Nationale, Paris. *Photo Larousse.*) *Below:* Statue of Louis XIII in the Place Royale (Place des Vosges). (Bibliothèque Nationale, Paris. *Photo Bulloz.*) *Opposite:* Comte de Montmorency-Boutteville, an early casualty of Richelieu's antidueling edict. (Musée du Louvre, Paris. *Photo Giraudon*)

FRANÇOIS DE MONTMORENCY 1622
COMTE DE BOUDEU.

IV

Conspiracy of the Ladies

Before the end of the cardinal's first eighteen months in office France and all Europe were put on notice that there was a statesman of the caliber of Henri IV at the Louvre. His intervention in the affair of the Valtelline marked the end of Spanish monopoly of northern Italy. His edicts against the *châteaux forts*, or walled castles, and against duels (the latter inspired by the death in a duel of his favorite brother, the marquis) demonstrated that he was not going to tolerate the continuation of the fun and games of feudalism. The comte de Montmorency-Bouteville, who defied the cardinal by killing a man in a duel in broad daylight in the Place Royale (now the Place des Vosges), was surprised and mortified to find himself mounting the scaffold, despite the impassioned pleas for mercy of half the nobility.

It took the latter a long time to grasp the fact that Richelieu meant what he said, and when they finally did, it took them an even longer time to learn that they could not get rid of him. For generations they had been allowed to plunder the countryside and to kill each other at will. The worst that could happen to them by way of discipline was a visit, more or less comfortable and accompanied by their own servants and silver, to the Bastille. Their rapacity was tempered only by a certain sense of dash and style and an occasional fit of religious fervor.

Anne of Austria by Philippe de Champaigne. (Collection Ulysse Moussalli. *Photo Bulloz*)

They were romantics who could never forgive Richelieu that he was not one of them. To them he was always a traitor to his class.

Far indeed from being a romantic, he was the strictest of classicists—in politics, in art, in life. His passion was form. Like the great château that he ultimately built at Richelieu, and the village that he erected at its gates, the nation that he sought to bring into being had to provide a perfect balance of the arts of war and peace, a symmetry of taste and glory. Richelieu saw France as contemporary allegorical painters in his employ came to see it, as represented by a warrior at whose feet were piled up the symbols of artistic creation and military conflict: on one side, an easel, a pen, a sculptor's tool; on the other, a shield, a spear, a cannon. On the brow, of course, were laurels.

The first conspiracy against Richelieu contained all the elements of *opéra bouffe* that one might have expected from his romantic opponents. They were like spoiled children at a private school indulging in a cabal against a stern headmaster whose true mettle they could never appreciate. The conspiracy grew out of the gossip and whisperings of three important ladies: the queen, Anne of Austria; her great friend, the duchesse de Chevreuse; and her cousin, the princesse de Condé.

Anne of Austria was Habsburg on both sides. On the paternal, she was a daughter of Philip III of Spain and a granddaughter of the terrible Philip II and of his fourth wife and own niece, another Anne of Austria. On the maternal, she was a daughter of Margaret of Austria, niece of the Emperor Maximilian II, her paternal grandmother's father. She was raised in the formal court at the Escorial, where every hour was controlled by a rigid etiquette, and dispatched as a young girl to a foreign court, permanently separated from her family, to become the bride of an unattractive and sullen youth who had no interest in her. By all our rules of heredity and environment, she should have turned into a psychological wreck. But the gift of life was strong in Anne. She had beauty and gaiety, and she delighted in the relative freedom of the French court. The brightest of the young nobility flocked to her, and she made a court within a court at the Louvre, as the young Marie-Antoinette was to do at Versailles a century and a half later.

What did such a creature care for the sober priest who was

taking charge of everything? What had she to fear from the domination of the Habsburgs? Anne maintained a secret correspondence with her brothers which must to her have seemed entirely natural but which Richelieu regarded as nothing less than treason. Two decades later, when she found herself regent of France for her infant son, Louis XIV, and the recipient of the wise counsels of Mazarin, she learned to be a Frenchwoman and a shrewd one. But that was after Richelieu's death. While he lived, and during the long years of her childlessness, there was no role for her in court but that of mischief-maker. This, however, was made amusing by the duchesse de Chevreuse.

Marie de Rohan-Montbazon was the most delightful woman of her day, and she has appropriately assumed the role of charmer in the nineteenth-century fiction where Richelieu plays the villain. Both in fiction and fact she was the very essence of what he was trying to tame in the French nobility. She was everything that Richelieu was not: beautiful, healthy, imaginative, sympathetic, romantic, witty. She cared nothing for crowns or laws but much for individuals and power. She was a brigand with a brigand's code of honor. Yet Richelieu was fascinated by her. Even knowing for a certainty that she hated him, he could never resist the delight of talking to her, of trying to win her over to his side. The very hopelessness of the task may have operated as a challenge.

Richelieu saw life in terms of discipline and order; Marie de Rohan saw it in terms of love and friendship. She had been married as a young girl to his old enemy, Luynes, and after his death to the much older duc de Chevreuse, of the house of Lorraine. She was constantly unfaithful to both husbands, but it was her remarkable quality to be able to remain on good terms with both lovers and spouses, and when an affair was over, she retained the lover as a friend for life. Richelieu's loyalty was to his country—he would decapitate any friend for it. Marie's was to her friends—she would blithely betray France for them. After her first real clash with him—following the collapse of the first conspiracy—she dedicated her life to his downfall. He sent her into exile, only to discover that she was more harmful abroad than at home. Duke Charles IV of Lorraine fell wildly in love with her; Philip

Claude de Lorraine, duc de Chevreuse.

Left: Henri de Talleyrand, comte de Chalais, victim of the *Conspiration des Dames.* (*Photo Larousse*). *Above:* César, duc de Vendôme, bastard son of Henri IV and Gabrielle d'Estrées. (Musée du Louvre, Paris. *Photo A. Giraudon*). *Opposite:* Marie de Rohan-Montbazon, duchesse de Luynes, later duchesse de Chevreuse, as Diana. (Musée de Versailles. *Photo Giraudon*)

Ce cerf a esté laissé courre et pris
au mont teincry par charles duc de
lorraine et de barle 15 juillet 1627

IV of Spain slept with her; Charles I of England became so attached to her that he actually stipulated the rescission of her banishment as one of his conditions to a treaty with France. Corneille's tragedies have many heroines of Marie's type. She was one of the last of the great individuals before the uniforming sweep of modern history.

The king and the cardinal had decided that Gaston, the king's brother, then eighteen and already converted to habits of dissipation, should marry the greatest heiress of France, Mademoiselle de Montpensier. Queen Anne objected to the match because she did not want Gaston to have a son and put her in the shade. It seems curious that she should have gone to any trouble to prevent what in those days was politically inevitable: the early marriage of the heir apparent to the throne, but she did. She and the duchesse de Chevreuse put their heads together to consider the best way to suborn Gaston. The princesse de Condé, whose husband was heir to the throne after Gaston, wished to keep the latter single as long as she could, so she joined them. The *Conspiration des Dames* was complete.

The three ladies began by winning to their party the man who had the greatest influence on Gaston, Ornano. Madame de Chevreuse then took upon herself the agreeable task of seducing a handsome young count, Chalais, an intimate of Louis XIII. The little clique grew. Soon it was having semitreasonable conversations with foreign ambassadors, and there was even some wild talk of shutting up the king in a monastery and declaring him impotent, both as husband and sovereign, so that his wife could marry the new king, Gaston. Richelieu soon detected the sand in the machinery of his royal matchmaking.

He acted quickly. Ornano was imprisoned in Vincennes. Gaston, furious, ran to the cardinal and demanded if he had advised the king to make this arrest. When Richelieu responded coldly that he had, Gaston muttered an obscenity and walked out. The conspiracy now spread to the bastard half brother of the king, the duc de Vendôme, and his brother, the grand prior of France. It was even decided to murder the cardinal, but at this point Chalais panicked and slipped the word to an uncle of his who warned Richelieu. The cardinal appeared at Gaston's levee and calmly handed him his shirt on the very morning

Gaston, duc d'Orléans, brother of Louis XIII and for twenty-eight years his troublesome heir apparent. (Bibliothèque Nationale, Paris. *Photo Larousse*)

Mademoiselle de Montpensier, "La Grande Mademoiselle," daughter of Gaston, duc d'Orléans, and niece of Louis XIII, by Mignard. (Private collection. *Photo Bulloz*)

when he was supposed to be at a spot where the conspirators could dispatch him. Gaston, thunderstruck, promptly deserted his colleagues, a way that was to become a habit, and made his own peace. He agreed to marry the heiress, so that a gift of the revenues of the greatest territory in France was his only punishment. The Vendôme brothers were locked up, and Chalais, who had gone back to the conspiracy after leaking it, paid for his disloyalty with his head.

The importance of the conspiracy was that it established permanently the hostility of the royal family to Richelieu. This was a menace that he had always thereafter to reckon with. The queen-mother saw her protégé giving orders to her favorite son. Gaston saw himself treated as the spoiled child he was. And the queen saw the place that she might have hoped to occupy at the side of her indifferent husband filled by a priest who seemed not only to control Louis but to see through her. A common detestation of the cardinal became the only bond between her and Marie de Médicis, but that bond was the greatest asset of the pro-Spanish party.

Despite Anne's overwhelming Habsburg background, Richelieu, with a little tact, might have won her over to French interests. After all, Mazarin, when she was a widow and regent, did. Mazarin knew how to handle women. A little proper attention from Richelieu, some appropriate flattery, might have found a welcome reception from Anne. She needed friends in the Royal Council. But Richelieu from first to last was hopeless with the other sex. The only thing he succeeded in doing with Anne was to temper her distaste with fear. Later he was to catch her red-handed in treasonable correspondence with Spain, and to threaten her harshly with repudiation and exile. Long after his death she would still tremble at his name and mutter that "that man" would be as powerful as ever if alive.

It was not that Richelieu underestimated the power of women. In a rueful entry in his memoirs he noted the extraordinary wrecking power that "these creatures" possessed. But he never learned to cope with them. When he tried to be gallant, he was heavy-handed; when he tried to instruct, he was pedantic. Although one of the principal architects of a Gallic civilization that became almost synonymous with the female genius, he never comprehended it. He always knew that the king's death would place him at the mercy of a sex that would soon dispose of him. It was appropriate that the first plot against him should have been the *Conspiration des Dames.*

Anne of Austria by Peter Paul Rubens. (Rijksmuseum, Amsterdam. *Photo Giraudon*)

George Villiers, First Duke of Buckingham. (National Portrait Gallery, London)

V

La Rochelle

The siege of La Rochelle was one of those great symbolic events that are seized upon by historians and students alike as evidence that there may be some logic in history. The beleaguered city has come to represent not only the principle of Protestantism in France but that of an independent middle class. It may even represent something not too far from democracy, at least as that word is defined under capitalism, something certainly more progressive than the royal absolutism of Louis XIII. For what did the besieging army represent but the principle of one crown, one church, and Gallic *gloire*, a philosophy that has even less currency today than the one that was starved out behind the walls of the maritime city? Moving the clock forward to 1685, the year of the revocation of the Edict of Nantes, and contrasting the forced emigration of thousands of skilled workers that followed that act of tyranny with all the nonsense of fancy dress that was then going on at Versailles, one has moments of wishing that Buckingham's fleet had, after all, been able to revictual the Protestant town.

But that is only one side of La Rochelle. It also represented separatism and the horrors which that implied in a world where religion to millions had become indistinguishable from murder and rapine. It represented piracy at sea, for it was a refuge for buccaneers. It represented the impotence of central government that gave the Habsburg powers leeway to do anything they wished beyond France's borders and

EMBARQUEMENT DU ROI, ET DU CA

Cum Privilegio Regis

A. Bosse

LE GALLIO

FLOTTANT

AVEC SES A

Allegorical print of the departure of Louis XIII and Richelieu for La Rochelle. (Bibliothèque Nationale, Paris. *Photo Giraudon*)

NAL DE RICHELIEU POUR LA ROCHELLE

N. DU ROY,

R L'OCCEAN,

GONAVTES.

The siege of La Rochelle, 1628. In the top part of the picture one can see the famous dike to the left. (Bibliothèque Nationale, Paris. *Photo Larousse*)

that guaranteed the great French nobles, Catholic and Protestant alike, immunity from royal discipline. Philip IV only pretended to give Spanish assistance to Richelieu in the subjection of the heretics. His Catholic Majesty saw to it that the promised naval aid was too little and too late. Similarly, the genial maréchal de Bassompierre, one of the queen-mother's party and an antiabsolutist, commented humorously on the folly of himself and his fellow peers in assisting the king and cardinal in their project: "Are we really going to be crazy enough to take La Rochelle?" For everybody saw the issue as clearly as historians have subsequently seen it—as crucial to the future of an ordered France.

One can sympathize today with the Huguenot minority that had learned to avoid massacre only by fortifying its towns and organizing its own armies. But there are still decisions in history that can be made only one way. The decision before the Huguenots was whether or not to bow to the crown and trust Richelieu to preserve the liberty of worship that he had promised them. They refused because they would not trust him. He was a cardinal, was he not? And even if sincere, was he not a mortal minister or at least a dismissable one? Was not the king a Catholic bigot? Was not the heir apparent? Who did not remember Saint Bartholomew's Day? Still, their decision was the wrong one. Richelieu *was* sincere and did allow them freedom of worship. They fought and died for nothing.

For France simply could not continue to exist as a nation with so many semiautonomous, fortified towns in her interior. The only thing a statesman could do was to pick the stronger party, suppress the weaker, and *then* establish tolerance. Richelieu was more an ancient than a modern Roman in his religious feelings. So long as his authority as first minister was recognized, his authority as a priest could pretty well go hang. And so long as the power of France was respected abroad, the power of Catholic France could go hang with the priest. If Richelieu overthrew the Huguenots at home, he also defeated the Counter Reformation abroad. A failure to recognize his twentieth-century common sense in matters of faith cost thousands of French Protestants their lives. He should, like Oliver Cromwell, have beseeched them, in the bowels of Christ, to consider that they might be mistaken.

In 1627 the duke of Buckingham precipitated the conflict. The great royal favorites of the seventeenth century, Lerma and Olivares, were superior in intellect to the sovereigns they dominated. Not so Buckingham. It was England's singular misfortune that this peacock should have enslaved the affections of both James I and Charles I, as Diane de Poitiers, more conventionally, had enslaved the affections of another royal father and son across the Channel. In Spain, on a ridiculous mission with Charles, then prince of Wales, to win for the latter the hand of an infanta, Buckingham had had the folly to offer his attentions to the wife of Olivares. In France, as the special ambassador delegated to escort to England Henrietta Maria, Louis XIII's sister, to be King Charles's queen, he dared to aim even higher. Anne of Austria had to call attendants because of his ardor one evening in a garden. After this Louis XIII refused to have him back in France, and some historians have given Buckingham's consequent pique as the reason for his per-suading his sovereign to outfit a fleet to bolster La Rochelle in its dis-pute with the French government. Others have argued that great historical events do not spring from such petty causes, but it is hard to see why not. Does an ass at the helm of the ship of state behave any less like an ass?

At any rate, when Buckingham appeared before La Rochelle with ten thousand-ton men-of-war and a hundred auxiliary vessels carrying an expeditionary force, it seemed the worst possible time for Richelieu. The king was ill. That terrible thorn in the side of France, the Protestant duc de Rohan, was raising the flag of rebellion in Languedoc. The dukes of Savoy and Lorraine were in arms. The troops of the emperor were operating close to the northeastern border. The royal bastion of Fort-Louis, just outside La Rochelle, was undermanned, be-cause its governor, Toiras, had sent many of its garrison to Fort-Saint-Martin on the island of Ré, which, with the island of Oléron, com-manded the sea approaches of the city. If Fort-Louis had been strongly attacked, it might have fallen, and La Rochelle would have been im-pregnable.

But Buckingham decided not to attack Fort-Louis. He decided

instead to land on the island of Ré and to attack Fort-Saint-Martin. According to Hilaire Belloc, this had been anticipated by Richelieu, who had reinforced Saint-Martin in the nick of time. Belloc goes almost as far as to attribute the ultimate salvation of France to the genius manifested in this decision. To other historians the reinforcement of Fort-Saint-Martin was a simple coincidence, or worse, the selfish act of Toiras, who wanted to protect his own interests in Ré. In any event, it ended in disaster for Buckingham because, although he succeeded in taking the island, he was unable to take Fort-Saint-Martin itself which the French royal forces, by great dexterity with small boats, were able to resupply. Eventually Buckingham had to evacuate the island, with much loss of life, and sail back to England, leaving La Rochelle with nothing but his promise to return.

The authorities of that city had hesitated before embarking on the treachery of an English alliance. When Rohan's brother, Soubise, had presented himself before the gates with an emissary of Charles I, he had found them closed to him. It had taken the violent pleas of his old warhorse of a mother, an object of the greatest veneration among the Huguenots, to overcome the prudence of the Town Council and to let him in. Now the townspeople saw the British fleet withdrawing and Louis XIII himself, with thirty thousand troops, approaching. But La Rochelle had guts enough for anything. Its spirit was expressed by its mayor, Guiton, who stuck his dagger in the council table and threatened to plunge it in the heart of the first to talk surrender.

Richelieu, before the walls, contemplated his prey. It would be necessary to close his eyes to the tumults in Germany, the deception of Savoy, the intrigues of Spain. Even in Languedoc, where the religious war continued, he would have to trust the dubiously loyal governor, Montmorency, to resist Rohan. He sent the latter's brother-in-law, Condé, to back him up, assuring himself of the latter's fidelity by the old Marie de Médicis technique of bribes. But there was no alternative. If Condé could just hold the line, Languedoc could be taken care of later. The siege would take at least a year, and Richelieu would not be able to leave the scene of action for so much as a day.

Everything depended on him. The generals quarreled over

precedence, and ultimately he had to take command himself. The king grew bored and returned to Paris, where he was subject to the influence of the queen-mother's cabal, but the risk had to be taken. The morale of the troops had to be supported by constant occupation and regular pay. And the passionate heroism of the besieged had to be met by a relentless ferocity that required the hanging of every soldier who allowed the least bit of succor to slip through the lines.

The town was at last tightly enclosed by seven miles of trenches, supported by twelve forts. But the mouth of the short canal that connected La Rochelle with the sea was just wide enough so that the royal batteries at either end were unable to prohibit marine traffic down the middle, and this hole, given the British supremacy at sea, threatened to be fatal unless plugged. The only thing to do was to build a dike to bridge the distance of almost a mile, leaving an open space in the middle for the passage of the tides, and this great work of engineering was undertaken simultaneously from both sides, under the personal supervision of Richelieu. Despite constant disheartening erosions by the violent sea the dike was at last completed, and La Rochelle was so effectively sealed off from all aid that the British fleet, when it did at last reappear, could do nothing but fire a few ineffective broadsides and sail away.

Victory was sure, but only if Richelieu could hang on till he had starved out the last rat-eater, the last cannibal. If this wretched town held out, all was lost. But if it fell—what an example! The lean, tired priest-warrior, pacing his dike and glancing toward the stubborn city, was surely concerned only that its sufferings might not be as bad as he prayed.

Opinion at last began to turn in his favor. The French clergy, assembled at Fontenay, voted three million livres to assist the king in his siege. The comte de Soissons, who was going to subvert Dauphiné and join Rohan, asked for a pardon. The duc de La Trémoille, the greatest Protestant peer of Poitou, abjured his faith. And La Rochelle was really starving at last. Even the old duchesse de Rohan was munching the harness from her carriage.

Just before the end, on September 30, 1628, the British fleet

Map of La Rochelle, showing the positions of the besieging
army. (Bibliothèque Nationale, Paris. *Photo Lauros-Giraudon*)

Above: Charles de Bourbon, comte de Soissons. Another prince of the blood whose immunity to the executioner's ax made him a constant pest to Richelieu. (*Photo Richard Kalvar/VIVA*). *Left:* Jean de Caylar de Saint-Bonnet de Toiras. (Bibliothèque Nationale, Paris. *Photo Larousse.*) *Opposite:* Louis XIII, Richelieu, and the maréchal de Bassompierre at the siege of La Rochelle. (La Sorbonne, Paris. *Photo Braun*). *Below:* Siege of La Rochelle: the dike. (Bibliothèque Nationale, Paris. *Photo Documentation Française-Holzapfel*)

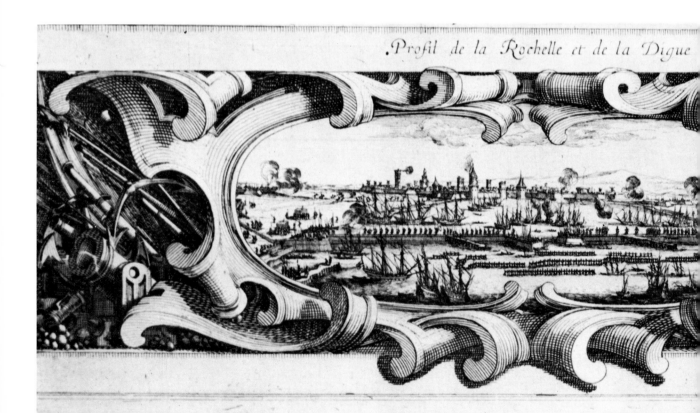

Profil de la Rochelle et de la Digue

Machine de duplessis et vassal

B

Louis XIII and Richelieu entering the surrendered city. The latter is supposed to have raised his head during the triumphal mass when its celebrant gave all the credit to God. (Musée d'Orbigny, La Rochelle. *Photo Giraudon*)

of one hundred and twenty sails made its last appearance. They faced a French fleet assembled in the canal; they faced a shore line covered with troops and cannon; they faced the king of France, back on the job; they faced Richelieu, in armor and red silk, standing on his dike. Behind, the walls of La Rochelle were covered with haggard, watching skeletons. There was some cannonading. Then the English were gone for good.

The town, reduced to a quarter of its original population of thirty thousand, capitulated, and on October 30 Richelieu, preceded by a convoy of supplies, rode into it. He expressed a formal dismay at the scenes of horror that greeted him, but one doubts if they did much to darken the fierce jubilation in his heart. When he asked the mayor what he thought of the kings of France and England, the weary old Huguenot replied that he preferred as a master the monarch who could take La Rochelle over him who could not defend it. The moment must have almost made up to the exhausted cardinal for a year of hideous anxiety.

The lesson taught at La Rochelle was soon learned all over the southern provinces of France where the Huguenots were still strong. After the first Italian campaign, in 1629, Richelieu left Suse with fifty thousand troops to clean up Protestant resistance in Languedoc and Guyenne. Rohan, desperate, had signed a treaty with the same king of Spain who was later to criticize Richelieu for cooperating with Gustavus Adolphus! The cardinal and Louis XIII met before the town of Privas whose inhabitants, guilty of many atrocities against Catholics, put up a desperate defense, despairing of royal clemency. Perhaps they were right to do so. Louis XIII had written to his mother: "These are Monsieur de Rohan's best men, and in hanging them all as I shall do, I shall be cutting off his right arm."

In the end, the exhausted town, as had La Rochelle, agreed to open its gates without conditions, but as the royal troops were entering, there was a powder explosion. Taking this as a sign of further resistance, they massacred a large part of the population. Richelieu, who was ill in his litter outside the walls, was careful in his memoirs to disassociate himself from this shameful deed. But no doubt he consoled himself at the shortening of civil war that such "involuntary rigor" might produce. Town after town now hastened to open its gates to the advancing army. Even the violent Montauban, which Luynes had been unable to take, the La Rochelle of the south, capitulated with shouts in the streets of "Long live the king and the great cardinal." Rohan had a conference with Richelieu and was allowed to go in voluntary exile to Venice. He would resist the king no longer, but he would not yet serve him.

By September of 1629, when Richelieu (after a triumphant tour through France in which all local governors were required to attend him in person) had rejoined the king in Fontainebleau, there had ceased to be an effective Huguenot resistance. He was ready at last to give his energies to the problems of France abroad.

Siege of La Rochelle. (*Photo Documentation Française-Holzapfel*)

Above: Siege of La Rochelle. (Musée du Louvre, Paris. *Photo Giraudon*) *Opposite:* Louis XIII congratulated by the merchants on his return from La Rochelle. (Bibliothèque Nationale, Paris. *Photo Larousse*)

Louis XIII, by Philippe de Champaigne. (The Prado Museum, Madrid. *Photo Giraudon*)

VI

Richelieu's Administrative Machinery

We complain today about the red tape of bureaucratic government, yet we can hardly conceive what it must have been like in the seventeenth century. The ailing Philip III of Spain was supposed to have suffered fatally from the overheating to which he was subjected when his armchair was placed too close to the fireplace at a time when the officer whose function it was to remove logs happened to be absent. Perhaps there was an ironic justice to his fate because the only efficient arm of his government was the Inquisition, and it had a proclivity for fires.

France was not as frozen in habit and custom as Spain, but she was very badly off. The administration of justice had no central authority; it was divided among eight *parlements* that had evolved from early assemblies of nobles and merchants into trial and appellate courts with hereditary functionaries. The greatest of these was the Parlement of Paris that had jurisdiction over half of France, but the seven other parlements—of Bordeaux, Dijon, Rennes, Rouen, Toulouse, Metz, and Pau—claimed exclusive jurisdiction over their local areas. It was a lawyer's paradise and a client's nightmare.

The Parlement of Paris had considerable political significance through its claim of discretion in recording. It was always insisting that if it had the power to record a royal edict, it had the power to refuse to do so—and that any such refusal operated as a veto on the crown. The king strenuously denied this and used a device known as the "bed of justice," when he summoned the Parlement of Paris to his presence, to enforce any tardy recordation. These jurisdictional conflicts were repeated, in lesser degrees, all the way down the social hierarchy between tax collectors and governors, towns and overlords, monasteries and squires, so that half the time of the courts was spent in determining whether or not they had the right to try the particular case before them. The disintegration of feudalism had created a bureaucratic chaos.

The executive authority was no clearer. France was divided into some thirty provinces ruled by governors who were usually great nobles with private armies of their own. Vast clerical properties were administered by powerful bishops and archbishops who were always looking over the heads of governor and king to a higher authority in Rome. The historian Michelet finds Richelieu's greatest failure in his inability to shift the burden of taxation from the poor to the nobles and clergy. Yet even Michelet admits that it might have been impossible.

Richelieu was first and last a practical man. He was not a political philosopher, and he made no fundamental changes in the governmental setup. He allowed the parlements to continue their clumsy administration of justice. He allowed taxes to continue to be raised from the poorest level of society by "tax farmers," who bought collection rights from the crown and collected far more than even the near confiscatory rates authorized. He allowed, in short, the whole vicious financial and legal system to go on as before, provided only that the edicts of Louis XIII were treated as the law of the whole land.

There is not a political idea or institution that comes down to us from Richelieu. He was an administrator, pure and simple. How one judges him in history must depend on whether one believes that he could have created a more flexible central authority and whether one believes that France could have survived his failure to create one at all. It is certainly arguable that he did the only thing that could be done in a dogfight: to smack the dogs on the noses with a strong stick. The more one contemplates the mess of France in 1624, the more it seems that only a rough policeman could have handled the job.

Richelieu, at any rate, had no doubts about the matter. From the beginning he believed that the authority vested in the crown was the only way out. He saw it as the only power in France that could be built up to contain the whole kingdom. And what else, in truth, was there? There was no background in France for any kind of representative government, assuming it to have been desired. Richelieu had one trump, the king, and he played it for all it was worth.

He had first to work on the man who occupied the sacred office. He minced no words. The business was too serious. Richelieu dared to lecture the king and his mother as if they had been students in a classroom. He had used language as flattering as that of any court sycophant when he was seeking power. But now that he had achieved it, and matters of national policy had to be discussed between the sovereign and his first minister, everything, including the king's feelings, had to be subordinated to them. In the famous address to Louis XIII after the victory of La Rochelle and before the first Italian expedition— a time of stern reappraisal of long-term objectives—Richelieu did not hesitate to tell his master that the latter was superficial in his judgments, that he was subject to fits of suspicion and jealousy, that he lacked assiduity and stick-to-it-iveness, that he had no proper sense of great objectives, that his aversions were sometimes irrational, and that he was ungrateful. It is surely a tribute to Louis' determination to succeed in his *métier du roi* that he took all this without a murmur.

Richelieu's plan was to extend the personality and authority of the king so that he would no longer, like a medieval overlord, have to travel all over his domain to get things done. The effective tool of the royal will was the King's Council. This did not meet as a single body. It was made up of several overlapping councils, such as the Council of Finance, Council of the Navy, Supreme Council, and so forth. The different councils met irregularly and at various places. Neither Louis nor Richelieu attended the meetings of those which took up the business of day-to-day government. The royal will was transmitted by a minister possessing the portfolio of "councilor to the king in all his councils." The chancellor, the keeper of the seals, and the two superintendents of finance each possessed this portfolio.

It must be understood that the councilors, at least after Richelieu was in charge of the appointments, were far from being pawns. They were brilliant, reasonable men who understood that Richelieu had put them where they were because he needed their advice, even though that advice might run counter to his own inclinations. Louis also valued independence of judgment, though, as we have seen at Suse, he sometimes lost his temper at its demonstration. He wrote Richelieu about Le Bouthillier when the latter became superintendent of finance:

> I believe you had better tell Monsieur Le Bouthillier to be firmer and stricter than he is with us. Otherwise he will grant everything we ask, and there will be no money left for the second half of the year.

De Bullion, Le Bouthillier's predecessor, a hearty man who, like most officials of the time, made a fortune in office, had never hesitated to say "no" to the first minister. Richelieu's understanding of finance and of currency problems was never deep, and he was inclined to be querulous when there was not enough money for his wars. De Bullion's minutes to him are common-sense assertions of the superiority of fiscal fact over political imagination.

The policies of the Council were carried out over the kingdom by intendants, who were simply crown representatives sent out from Paris to supervise the local administration of a particular edict. Sometimes they might be sent to conduct an investigation or even, as in the case of Laubardemont at Loudun, to conduct a criminal trial. They were mere executive arms, but their importance was that they outranked the local governor. There had been intendants before Richelieu, but he developed their functions into a coordinated administrative system. Naturally, they were much resented by local magnates, and the word "intendant" became synonymous with autocratic oppression from Paris.

In the case of a man as busy as Richelieu it was inevitable that his friends should have been selected from among his co-workers. Unquestionably the greatest of these, both in intimacy and ability, was the Capuchin monk, père Joseph (François Le Clerc du Tremblay), a nobleman and soldier turned mystic and priest, who met Richelieu early in his career and had attached himself to the younger man. They were a strange team. Père Joseph was rough, hard, and ruddy, a man devoted to the plainest living and highest thinking. Richelieu was frail, fine, and subtle, and he cared about luxury and high rank. The Capuchin had an

Père Joseph, the "Gray Eminence." (*Photo Giraudon*)

obsession with a crusade to rescue the Holy Land. He was always looking for money and troops for this visionary ideal, and he wrote a long,
unreadable epic poem on the subject entitled the "Turkiad." Richelieu,
on the other hand, limited himself entirely to practical objectives and
probably would have cared little about the Holy Land even had its
liberation been feasible. Père Joseph was deeply, ecstatically religious,
whereas the cardinal was simply an orthodox Catholic. It may have been
a case of the attraction of opposites. But it is also clear that once père
Joseph had been convinced by Richelieu that the interests of the church
(and of any ultimate crusade) were identical with the temporal interests
of the French monarchy, he placed a tough, agile mind, an infinite in-
dustry, and an unquestionable loyalty at the cardinal's service.

Père Joseph became one of the four secretaries of state and was
used primarily in diplomacy. He traveled to Germany and to Italy, at
first on foot in the tradition of the Capuchins but ultimately (no doubt
at Richelieu's orders) in a state carriage. He was a strange combination
of simplicity, even naïveté, with shrewdness and toughness. It must
have made him very difficult to penetrate or predict. He seems to have
effected a complete dichotomy between God and this world, so that
he was able to renounce all temptations of the flesh with the ease of a
mystic and, at the same time, to send men to their deaths without a
qualm. He understood both the sophistication of courts and the allure
of monastic cells. Being without an ax to grind, he was more trusted
than Richelieu and far more popular. Louis XIII and Gaston, for example, were both devoted to him. And being without vanity—at least
of the obvious variety—he had the added value of being repudiatable.
Richelieu could disavow père Joseph's acts, as he did with the Regensburg Treaty, without offending him.

A very real friendship seems to have united the two men. There
is a legend that Richelieu, attending the deathbed of his friend in his
own château at Rueil, offered him the final consolation of the news of
the fall of Breisach to France's allies—although this event did not
occur until after père Joseph's demise. One would like to think the
story were true. It throws a pleasant light on the cardinal. What is more
certainly true is that père Joseph, who had none of Richelieu's nervous-

ness and who probably did not know what fear was (except, perhaps, fear of hell-fire, a constant preoccupation of the times), offered his friend on occasion a much needed bucking up. In the terrible year 1636, when the Spaniards seemed about to fall upon Paris, Richelieu temporarily lost his head. It was père Joseph who brought him around and induced him to drive through the streets without his guard to allay the fears of a population on the verge of panic. It must have given great consolation to the harassed cardinal to know the availability of that strong, homely, faithful presence, to feel the totality of that intelligent and friendly interest devoid of envy and spite. In 1638 Richelieu asked for a cardinal's hat for his friend, but père Joseph died before it came. Perhaps it was just as well. It is hard to imagine him in the splendid trappings of a prince of the church.

Two other intimates of the Council were the Le Bouthilliers, father and son. Their connection went far back, for Claude Le Bouthillier, the father, appears to have had some legal connection, perhaps a partnership, with Richelieu's lawyer-grandfather, La Porte. The family, at any rate, was totally devoted to Richelieu, who used Claude and his son, Léon, for the most delicate and confidential jobs.

The son, who became more important than the father, is known to history by the title of comte de Chavigny. As early as 1632, when he was only twenty-five years old, he was one of the secretaries of state. He seems to have acted as a spy for his master in households that were hostile or potentially hostile. Thus, as a young man he served as a secretary to the queen-mother, and in 1635 he was made chancellor of Gaston's household. Chavigny must have been a man of some hidden charm, or at least of imposing personality, for Gaston seems to have liked him, even though he was guilty of such intemperate conduct as of once seizing a button on Gaston's vest and exclaiming: "I want you to know that the cardinal can make you shake when he wishes, just as I shake this button!" Perhaps Gaston, who never lost his sense of humor, thought this was funny. He seems always to have enjoyed the company of his handsome, somber, brilliant, and untrustworthy chancellor.

Chavigny fulfilled the great condition to Richelieu of absolute devotion. He described the cardinal as "the only man I regard as master and for whose obedience I profess a blind passion." He was capable of violent extravagance and dissipation and of equally violent fits of remorse. It is not surprising that he ended his days as a Jansenist. But the cardinal never minded extravagance or arrogance in his underlings so long as they were devoted to his interests and willing to work hard and effectively when he needed them. He molded Chavigny into a perfect instrument for his purposes, but one that was good for nobody else. After the cardinal's death, poor Chavigny proved completely unusable to Mazarin. He died prematurely and out of office. It was said that he was Richelieu's son, but this would have been said of any younger intimate of the first minister. To the gossips of the court, there were two explanations for such a relationship: the favored person was either a bastard or minion. But the cardinal was always willing to let people talk—if they only talked.

Léon Le Bouthillier, comte de Chavigny.

Louis XIII receiving Claude Le Bouthillier into the Order of the Holy Ghost. (Musée des Augustins, Toulouse. *Photo Giraudon*)

C. oorrand fecit eccudit

Engraving from 1627 showing Richelieu as superintendent of navigation and commerce. (Bibliothèque Nationale, Paris. *Photo Giraudon*)

VII

Richelieu's Personality

One of the difficulties in getting a clear picture of Richelieu is the obfuscation caused by the literary legend. From Dumas, Hugo, and Alfred de Vigny, right down to the Hollywood script-writers of the 1930s, the cardinal is shown as a Machiavellian villain, utterly remorseless, and without scruple. In *Marion Delorme* he is too spooky a creature even to be allowed to appear on stage. A huge closed litter is carried across the set from the interior of which a muffled "No mercy" is heard in sole response to the desperate pleas of his kneeling victims. In the Dumas novels his scarlet robe, flashing from palace to castle, is as much a part of the action as the clashing swords of the musketeers. In later Victorian days this image was softened by Bulwer-Lytton whose readers were given a peek at a darling old gentleman with a heart of gold lurking behind the mask of the iron statesman, a conception brought to later generations of theatergoers by E. H. Sothern and Walter Hampden. Yet the outwardly stern cardinal, which even these interpreters showed to their stage enemies, was very much the same as the one pictured by the romantic French novelists. The very name "Richelieu" has become a synonym for hammy historical drama.

On the other hand, the Richelieu of the memoirs of his contemporaries is an equally inaccurate picture. These were generally the works of noblemen high up in the social scale who, for the reasons that we have seen, detested the cardinal. It was not a day when accuracy of recording was much in vogue, and the most scandalous rumors were set down with relish. We see in these pages a first minister who thought only of enriching himself and his family, who used poison as widely and skillfully as the Italian villain of a Jacobean tragedy, who hampered

Richelieu wearing the Order of the Holy Ghost, artist unknown. (Musée de Richelieu. *Photo Richard Kalvar/VIVA*)

the careers of great poets if they wrote better verse than he, and who lusted after young women, even including Queen Anne. In all this mound of dreary spite there is hardly a tale that is even amusing, and so it is a relief to come across this one: when Richelieu's niece, Madame de Combalet, heard the rumor spread by the maréchal de Brézé that her brother's four children were really her own and sired by her cardinal uncle, she complained indignantly to the queen who replied with a giggle: "But we never believe more than half of what Brézé says!"

Let us make a start, anyway, in our attempt at characterization, by studying the great full-length portrait by Philippe de Champaigne. This Brussels painter, who became a Jansenist, took to portraits to avoid painting nudes. Certainly, no artist has ever used robes to greater effect. The tall, lissome figure of the cardinal seems to glide before us, a symbol of aristocratic authority. Now he appears to pause. He has noted us; we have brought something to mind. Those cold, clear, appraising eyes give us our exact due—no more, no less. The cardinal knows well enough when to praise, when to flatter, when to yield, but such attitudes are not for the likes of us. Have we understood our mission? Is it perfectly clear? Very well. Let us be sure we perform it. And the rustling robes move on. The face that we have seen is uniquely cerebral. Champaigne accomplishes his effect by a combination of triangles: the long bony tapering nose, the pointed chin and beard, the white lapel of the collar, the creases in the arras, the blue sash of the order of the Holy Ghost, the white surplice, and others, all through the red robe.

But this, of course, is a portrait. Champaigne aimed at showing his subject at his strongest. One is convinced that the cardinal sometimes looked that way, but not always. It would never have done to have shown a weaker moment. It would never have done, for example, to have shown him in tears, which by all reports he frequently was, or in full gallop down the corridors of the Palais-Cardinal, whinnying and snorting, on the rare evenings when, according to a legend handed down in the French royal family, he imagined himself to be a horse.

Did he ever? Probably not. Yet there was surely madness in his family. His brother Alphonse, whom he dragged from a monastery to make cardinal-archbishop of Lyon, had periods when he imagined himself God the Father, and his sister Nicole, who suffered from the delusion that her backside was made of glass, had eventually to be put away. But it seems more likely that in Armand the family failing manifested itself merely in periodic depressions and fits of temper, and in the weeping that we have noted. Even some of these may have been simulated for a political purpose. Marie de Médicis observed sourly that he could turn his tears on and off as he chose.

At first blush there seems a contradiction between Richelieu's courage and dignity in the large and his nervousness and irritability in the small. On one hand we see the warrior priest who braved the heavy seas and enemy shells to supervise the building of the great dike at La Rochelle, who led an army over snowy passes into Italy, who refused to give in to the pro-Spanish peace party at court even when the king's life seemed to hang by a hair, who looked death in the eye when it came and told his confessor that his only enemies were those of France. On the other we see the man who would inspect all the corners of the room before he went to bed, who was so closely guarded that one had to pass through five different groups of musketeers to reach his chamber, who sobbed when he was excited, and who flew into violent tantrums over trifles and sometimes struck his servants. The answer may be found in the terrible strain that his work load imposed on his ever-frail health. It had to be sustained by will power alone.

At twenty-two, when he became bishop of Luçon, he was already afflicted with intermittent fevers. From 1611 onward he suffered from migraines, which were the torment of his life. According to the notes of his doctor, in one bout of illness in 1635 he had seventy-five enemas, together with innumerable pills and laxatives. Three years earlier he almost died of a retention of urine. He had to endure ulcers, rheumatism of the jaw, chronic constipation, and agonizing hemorrhoids. An operation on the latter resulted in a near-fatal abscess. Anne of Austria and her coterie referred to him in their correspondence as *"Cul Pourri."* But worst of all was a tubercular osteitis of the right arm which caused suppurations that must have at times made it difficult for councilors to sit at the same table with him. On his deathbed, when all medical hope was gone, the desperate remedy of an old peasant woman's panacea was tried: horse dung macerated in white wine. As Aldous Huxley put it: "It was with the taste of excrement in his mouth that the arbiter of Europe's destinies gave up the ghost."

Richelieu, in view of the foregoing, was not being just foxy in 1629, after La Rochelle, when he delivered his famous harangue to the king and the queen-mother about how those in charge of the state would have to behave. If he were going to go on with the job, he warned them, everybody, including the king, was going to have to straighten out. For the task might otherwise be too much for him:

> If I could cure my body of its ills as easily as my spirit of its faults, I should be much comforted. I would no longer have to ask Your Majesties to take into account my wretched health. But every day I am aware of the ebbing of essential strength. It is indeed a terrible responsibility to have to conduct the affairs of a great nation when one is constantly undermined by physical suffering.

All observers agreed that Richelieu could be charming when he wanted to, and as he had constantly to be bargaining—with great nobles, with high clerics, with parliamentarians, with ambassadors, and crowned heads—he must often have wanted to. He spoke Latin, Greek, Italian, and Spanish, and his arguments were clear, cogent, convincing, and delivered in a gracious and pleasing manner. To what extent they were enhanced by any warmth of personality it is difficult to say. It does not appear that the cardinal had any great gift for affection. He probably succeeded in making himself genuinely fond of the king. Certainly he must have cared for père Joseph. And he had much kindness for those of his household who were totally devoted to his interests. But what master would not have? The fact seems to be that he did not need other people as most of us do. His heart was too full of himself and the glory of France.

With regard to women, there is not one speck of dependable evidence that he ever had a love affair. Undoubtedly he felt the charm

Cardinal Richelieu by Philippe de Champaigne. (Musée du Louvre. *Photo Giraudon*)

"The Majority of Louis XIII" by Peter Paul Rubens. (Musée du Louvre. *Photo Giraudon*)

of the duchesse de Chevreuse, the most dazzling creature of her day, for he seems to have liked talking to her, even when he knew that she was plotting against his very life. In his later years ill health probably cooled any sexual urges, and in his early ones a serious regard for his clerical vows may have kept him chaste. Not all clergymen were gallants. And it is fairly certain that if, as first minister, living as he did with hundreds of retainers watching him day and night, with secretaries even sleeping in his bedroom, he had had affairs, we should have heard of them. That the gossips were reduced to coupling his name with those of his own niece and the queen of France may have shown how desperate they were.

Richelieu had one blind spot which gained him many unnecessary enemies. He could never understand how wounding his tongue could be. This probably sprang from a deficiency of the imagination, an inability to place himself in other people's shoes. When he sent Bassompierre to the Bastille, he wrote him a letter of priestly advice requesting that every tenth Hail Mary that he said in prison should be offered for Richelieu himself! "If you find this too much," he went on, "I shall be content with every twentieth, for one Hail Mary said with devotion is worth more than thirty said with distraction." This remarkable letter has been interpreted, quite naturally, as one of cruel sarcasm to a helpless prisoner, but the more one reads of the cardinal's correspondence, the more one suspects that it was perfectly sincere. Richelieu, like most who lack a sense of humor, was inclined to be literal. He probably did not understand, when he called jovially to the freakishly ugly marquis de Fontrailles to ask him to leave the audience chamber before an ambassador arrived, because the latter did not care for "monsters," that he had added a plotter to a future conspiracy against himself.

Again and again we find him indulging this inclination to make cutting remarks, even at the cost of important friends. When the lay cardinal de Guise renounced the wealthy archbishopric of Rheims to marry Marguerite de Gonzague, Richelieu exclaimed to him: "What, you would give up an income of four hundred thousand livres for a woman? Most men would give up four hundred thousand women for your income!" But his insensitivity to the feelings of others did not keep him from being easily hurt himself. On the second expedition to relieve Casale Monferrato, when the army approached Turin through rain and mud, Richelieu heard himself roundly cursed as his carriage passed the trudging foot soldiers. He stopped to complain to a major. The poor officer replied that this sort of thing had to be expected from weary men under the circumstances. "But you should forbid it!" the cardinal cried. Presumably the major saluted and sighed with relief as the carriage passed on.

Richelieu's obtuseness to his fellow beings went back to his early days. As bishop of Luçon writing to the comtesse de Soissons on the occasion of her husband's death, he offered the following cold comfort:

> If you are truly desirous of your own well-being, you should recognize that it is better to have an advocate in heaven than a husband on earth.

Such failure of imagination, which often accompanies the most prodigious powers of deduction and analysis, made the cardinal a bit heavy-handed in the lighter moments of life. So we see him, in a playful mood, asking the abbé de Boisrobert, the poet who acted as a kind of unofficial jester, what he supposed gave his master the greatest pleasure in life. "Making France happy and prosperous, my lord?" came the flattering suggestion. "No, making verses!" came back the fatuous rejoinder.

The Princesse Palatine, a daughter of the duc de Nevers, gives an amusing incident of this weightiness in the cardinal. She describes a meeting at the hôtel de Rambouillet where there was a discussion of the nature of love. Mademoiselle de Scudéry told the gathering of a friend of hers, violently enamored, who had been obliged to go abroad and leave his mistress for a time. He had spoken of the agony of parting in expressions so touching that Mademoiselle de Scudéry had wept to hear him. But the duc d'Enghien, as the son and heir of the prince de Condé was always known (this one was later the *Grand* Condé), took the opposing position that a man so concerned with the mere expression of his love could be no true lover at all. The company was much struck by his argument, which was widely discussed afterward in society. Word of it came to the cardinal. He promptly planned a dinner at Rueil and invited all those who had taken part in the discussion at the hôtel de Rambouillet. Armchairs were arranged in a circle, and the cardinal asked the Princesse Palatine's sister to act as president of the assembly. The matter was conducted with the gravity and dignity of a royal council where the destiny of an empire was at stake. The duc d'Enghien repeated his sentiments. His sister, the future duchesse de Longueville, took the other side, and Mademoiselle de Scudéry acted as advocate general. The Princesse Palatine describes the result as follows:

> The cardinal took everybody's vote. When it was my turn, I declared for the duc d'Enghien and said that I regarded subtle expressions and distinctions of tenderness as so much fol-de-rol. My opinion decided the cardinal, and the duc d'Enghien was as much pleased by his triumph as if it had been one of his victories in the field. I was much flattered by our host, who had from the beginning been for the opinion of the duc d'Enghien. It may seem astonishing that the cardinal would so dignify such a topic and such an assembly, but that was the spirit of the times and particularly his. The sublime genius which could balance the destinies of empires, which could cast an eagle eye over all of Europe, which could make such bold decisions and follow them up with such persistence, deserted Richelieu the moment it came to private discussion. Then he showed himself pedantic and formalistic. In his retirement at Avignon he had written a treatise about divine love with metaphysical subtlety; now he brought the same method to profane love. Anybody else would have seemed absolutely ridiculous, but so much glory surrounded him and so much splendor was spread over the least of his actions, that we regarded these pedantries and college dissertations on a subject so inappropriate for them as the vagaries of a great mind occupied with matters sublime.

There is an unintentional snobbishness in historians of the period who are almost unanimous in judging the cardinal (sometimes with admiration) as a merciless and revengeful man. This reputation is largely based on his execution of certain great noblemen who, by modern standards, almost without exception deserved death. Suppose a member of the cabinet of any European nation today were to conspire with a foreign power to bring about the fall of his chief. Does anybody think he would go free if caught and convicted? Yet no one of the cardinal's more famous victims—Montmorency, Chalais, Cinq-Mars—did anything much less.

Before Richelieu there had been a different law for the mighty and for the small. The great nobles had little to occupy themselves but to engage in cabals against the crown in the expectation, too often justified, of being able to call off a threatened or actual mutiny in return for increased estates or greater pensions. And it was understood that this was a perfectly respectable occupation. The queen-mother herself did not hesitate to make war on her son to obtain certain privileges for her household. But, of course, as these conspiracies usually involved some degree of treasonable correspondence with a foreign power, usually Spain, somebody had to pay for them, and a few poor clerks or army officers were broken on the wheel. All that Richelieu did was to carry the death penalty to the top, where it belonged. He made it clear that these games would no longer be considered games. He put an end to the masked-ball aspect of civil disunion.

In England there had been no such nonsense. If a prince of the blood led a rebellion, retribution started with him. Even a crown did not save its wearer from the scaffold, as Mary Stuart had discovered. If Richelieu had been able to execute Gaston, half the conspiracies of his administration might have been avoided. He was constantly plagued by the immunity of the blood royal and by the king's malicious willingness to lend an ear to chatter against his first minister which misled courtiers into thinking that he might tolerate more overt acts of insubordination.

Unlike his master, Richelieu was never cruel. He was merciless because he thought that mercy incited disorder. Once he had decided that a man had to be executed for the good of the nation, he did not care if a sufficient crime were proved against him. Marillac, the victim of a judicial lynch, is the obvious example of this. On the other hand, Richelieu's tolerance of the Protestants after their cause had been lost was probably dictated by equally cold reasons of policy. So long as the end justified the means—and a strong, unified France was always his

Louis XIII. (Bibliothèque Nationale, Paris. *Photo Giraudon*)

Petrus Daret *sculpsit.*   1647

end—it did not matter what those means were. They might be bloody or not. The most effective would be chosen—that was all.

The cardinal's faith in his goal gave him enormous strength against his enemies. He might have been nervous and jumpy about day-to-day risks, but he was absolutely unwavering about the necessity for his undergoing them. He identified his life with the glory of France. There was no question in his mind that he had to control and direct the state, by fair means or foul, so long as he had a breath in him. This was his clear duty to an orderly France and to an orderly God. He could never even consider compromising with the Spanish party—even by an inch—and thus saving his own neck in case of the king's death. He was heroic by long-range standards, if timid by short. Those who hated him were not *his* enemies. They were traitors to the state.

Yet, ironically enough, Richelieu's reputation for bloodiness, if not justified by the execution of rebels, is quite justified by other, less publicized deaths. Because men like Chalais and his successors went to their merited deaths with courage and style, the cardinal in history seems as red as his robes. But the untold thousands, if not millions, who died horribly in Germany because of his deliberate policy of continuing the Thirty Years' War are not usually held to his account, or at least were not, before Aldous Huxley's brilliant indictment in *Grey Eminence.* Until our own times a statesman was considered perfectly justified in building his nation's prosperity on the havoc of others.

126

The Bernini bust. (*Photo Richard Kalvar/VIVA)*

VIII

Richelieu's Routine and Household

Richelieu's daily habits, like his personality, have been obscured by his legend. One tends to think of him as a scarlet presence standing always just behind the king or following the latter grimly through a double line of bowing courtiers. Now it is perfectly true that hardly a day could go by without Richelieu's informing himself as to what the king was doing and particularly as to whom he was seeing, be it a Jesuit confessor, a royal relation, or a strapping musketeer, but that did not have to mean that Louis XIII and his first minister spent all their time in the same domicile. Had the cardinal accompanied the king simply on his hunts, he would have lacked time to get through his tasks. Furthermore, a constant companionship would have exposed the king to too much of the tension of feeling his own mental capacities overcast by those of his brilliant adviser. Richelieu could temper this at scheduled meetings with pleasant manners and flattery, but no man could be a courtier all day, every day and still govern France.

No, it was necessary that the two be near but not together, which was why Richelieu established himself in his château at Rueil, close to the favorite royal residence of Saint-Germain, and in Paris in the Palais-Cardinal down the street from the Louvre. Correspondence went back and forth between them daily, but meetings were less frequent. The kind of devotion that they had for each other—and it existed—probably flourished best in memory and reflection.

The cardinal's routine was designed to enable an ailing man to get through a formidable work load. Purely social matters were rigidly eliminated. Richelieu did not turn up at court balls and ballets unless

On horseback. (Bibliothèque Nationale, Paris. *Photo Giraudon*)

there was a special reason. He would not even receive ambassadors unless there was a particular matter to discuss, and personal interviews for private persons, even great ones, were notoriously difficult to obtain. The cardinal used the Louvre as a modern prime minister uses Buckingham Palace—to work off the ceremonial side of business and leave him free for the real labor.

After an ordinary workday, Richelieu went to bed at eleven at night, and slept for three or four hours. He would then call for a light and his portfolio and would write or dictate to the secretary who slept in his room. This secretary had to dress his abscesses as well. The cardinal usually went back to sleep at six o'clock and arose between seven and eight. After prayers, the four regular secretaries would enter, and he would dictate dispatches that he had noted the night before. These secretaries were selected for their efficiency in transcribing dictation and for their discretion. Their duties were mechanical, for Richelieu was satisfied with his own language and wanted no editing. But a single indiscretion, and they were fired. So successful was their master in this respect that none of them, even after his death, wrote a word about their employment. They were probably not very interesting men.

This kind of secluded, industrious existence promoted, in the needs of relaxation, a kind of one-way intimacy with the principal members of the household. Once Richelieu was absolutely convinced of their loyalty, once he was satisfied that they had become minor extensions of his own personality, he could, like other melancholy and lonely great men, become almost embarrassingly playful. He would assail them through a peashooter, throw books at their heads, yawn elaborately when they were talking, pinch them, prick them, or tickle them. He liked to organize elaborate practical jokes, such as having them robbed by fake thieves or printing fake gazettes containing uncomplimentary articles about them. A favorite game in the great hall during recesses was to line up with backs against the wall and see who could jump the highest. The duc de Gramont, happening to enter the chamber while Richelieu was so engaged, proceeded imperturbably to take his place in the line and to jump with the others.

The cardinal, in his constant journeys through France, traveled with almost as large a retinue as the king. In addition to his hundred horse guards, and as many musketeers, he was accompanied by a household of a hundred and eighty. Wagonloads of provisions with the kitchen and bedchamber staff went ahead to prepare the lodging at the next stop. In the room selected for the cardinal his own furniture and tapestries were arranged, and by the time he arrived, everything was in order, with musketeers stationed, watches set, meals prepared, as in his houses in Paris or Rueil. This was in marked contrast to the sloppiness of the royal household on the same journeys where Louis XIII had on occasion to dine at an uncovered table or even sleep in an unmade bed.

Richelieu's personal train resembled a small army. We have a glimpse of him leaving Rueil on a voyage in 1639 to Champagne and to Lyon. In the center of the convoy was borne the litter that he would use when the roads were too rough for his aches and pains. But on this first day of the trip he is feeling better and occupies the right-rear seat in a carriage drawn by six horses. Through the open window he glances at the green banks of the Seine under the spring morning mist, and from time to time his thin, bony fingers touch a volume in his lap, richly bound in red morocco with a dedication on the cover in gold letters. It is the *Armaneïde*, a poem composed in his praise which the author has presented to him that morning at his levee. At his side, the abbé de Beaumont is deep in his breviary. Facing them, two members of the household, one with a great portfolio in red leather on his lap, quietly chat. At the cardinal's door rides a guard with a drawn sword in hand. Two grooms and two gentlemen servants canter just behind. On all sides the horse guards are posted. They are followed by carriages with members of the cardinal's entourage and the heavy wagon bearing the silver and plate. In the rear ride the pages. When the procession arrives at the first stage of the journey, the cardinal's carriage passes ahead to his lodging between two rows of saluting musketeers who have been in the advance party.

The cardinal continues to govern France on the journey. He must, for he will be gone six months. Consider the communications borne by his courier. From Pontoise he carries: specific orders to the procurer-general for suppression of the disorders at the abbey of Saint-Savin, military instructions to the generals in the Low Countries and in Italy; memoranda relating to the intrigues of the duchesse de Chevreuse; a note to the French ambassador in Switzerland about the Grisons; letters concerning the treaty with the landgrave of Hesse and the loss of the Battle of Thionville. From Abbeville, the courier carries further letters dealing with the war on the Spanish border and with the ransoms to be negotiated with the emperor's general, Piccolomini; instructions for the punishment of those derelict in duty at the siege of Thionville; suggestions about engaging a Spanish flotilla due in from the West Indies; orders about the siege of Hesdin; orders about the heading off of a certain duel threatened between two nobles; and, finally, a letter about one of his own devotional works: *Of the Perfection of a Christian.* So it goes, throughout the long and tedious voyage. Whether it be a question of a siege, a battle, a tax, the suppression of a rebellion, the uncovering of a plot, the regulation of a nephew's household, the grant of a pension to a poet, the plan of a ballet for a party—all receive the due attention of the all-probing mind.

The cardinal took great pride in the military establishment which the king had granted him after the Chalais conspiracy. Louis XIII did not want to lose so valuable a minister to an assassin's knife, but at the same time he was constantly jealous that a mere subject should have a guard, even one of his own concession. Tactful as the cardinal ordinarily was in his relations with the king, his own fear of violent death, added to his conviction that a display of force was the best deterrent, plus also, perhaps, a strong personal vanity that was satisfied by a military escort, led him into many unnecessary embroilments with the Louvre. The guards at the Palais-Cardinal wore red tunics with white crosses to distinguish them from the royal musketeers, but this only intensified a rivalry that found its echo in Dumas' novels. The cardinal liked to have all his horse guard accompany him about Paris, and on one occasion he actually requested that some of his guards escort him into the royal courtyard at Saint-Germain. The king, of course, refused, but it is sufficiently striking that Richelieu presumed even to ask. Nothing disgusted the king more, when he went to the

Palais-Cardinal, than to see all the bustle of the guards and servants in the courtyard. "Go ahead of me!" he snapped once at his minister as they were about to enter the palace. "You are evidently more king here than I!" Richelieu responded with a quick wit to what might have been a crisis. He took the torch from a page and raised it high as he respectfully preceded the king. "Only to light your way, Sire," he replied. But Louis XIII was to have the last word. Leaving the Palais-Cardinal on his final visit to the dying Richelieu, he stationed his own musketeers at all the entrances. "Never again," he was heard to mutter, "will I have a favorite with guards."

It was not only the king who found the atmosphere of the cardinal's habitations unduly military for a priestly home. François Ogier, the famous preacher, invited to perform this office before the cardinal, describes the occasion as follows:

> I preached in a chamber that was unfamiliar to me, but it was certainly not a chapel. A large square formed by musketeers created an empty space between the chair of the preacher and that of the cardinal. The latter, properly speaking, was not a chair at all. It was more a throne, raised on a dais, and round it thronged dukes, peers and secretaries of state. Happy the chevalier who could so much as touch its back while the captain of the guards was looking the other way! My surplice got caught in a soldier's halberd; the odor of wicks and powder assailed my nostrils. . . .

Richelieu's work schedule at home was necessarily interrupted by a certain minimum of entertainments which had to be offered to the visiting great or to the king himself. Dinner, the principal meal of the day, which took place in mid-afternoon, was the most convenient occasion for these, and we see one as reconstructed by a student of the cardinal's household, Maximin Deloche.

The table is set for fourteen, with spotless, glistening, white table linen and a meticulously spaced array of dishes and goblets. The neatness and cleanness of the service are all the more noted in a day when it is still common for the highest of the land to spit on the floor and when some of the remnants of previous meals are not infrequently to be detected on the table. The cardinal was determined to establish

Richelieu saluting the infant dauphin (the future Louis XIV). An interesting meeting between the two architects of French royal absolutism. (Bibliothèque Nationale, Paris. *Photo Documentation Française*)

in his own household the order and harmony that he hoped to extend throughout France. The napkins are ingeniously folded to suggest an anchor, symbol of Richelieu's portfolio, never delegated, of the navy. After the birth of the future Louis XIV, they will be shaped, for a time, as dolphins. When the guests have taken their places, still standing, a benedicite is uttered. As they take their seats, the cardinal glances about, like an inspecting officer, to assure himself that everything is in order. If so, his thin lips are briefly pursed in satisfaction. Dinner is in three services: (1) *hors d'œuvre*, soup, *entrée*; (2) roasts, salad, *entremets*; (3) further *entremets*, and then a dessert in which the genius and fancy of Daicq, the *maître d'hôtel*, are given full rein. The latter, the artist of the occasion, presides, efficiently but tensely, over the repast. Sword at side, hat on head, he leads the splendid procession of waiters bearing each service into the chamber, and then takes his place behind the cardinal's chair. Two pages, stationed at his sides, attend to the great man's needs, but it is Daicq himself who presents the napkin when Richelieu has rinsed his fingers at the end.

From contemporary records we have a glimpse of the cardinal at one of his greater entertainments: a production of Scudéry's *L'Amour Tyrannique* in the hall which accommodated six hundred persons but which would later be used only for rehearsals after Lemercier had added a proper theater to the Palais-Cardinal. The abbé de Boisrobert is in charge of the invitations, and two gentlemen of the household, the chief groom and the captain of the musketeers, carefully check every name against a master list. Boisrobert has no wish to repeat the disgrace that he suffered when Gaston (of all people!) was able to point out gleefully to the cardinal that a notorious prostitute had obtained a bid to one of his parties. Tonight, after the final verses, with their compliments to the king, the audience rises to applaud and cheer the new dauphin. The bishop of Auxerre, followed by twenty pages carrying the supper on heavy trays of silver gilt, heaped with sweetened lemons, orange confections, and every imaginable fantasy of pastry, approaches the royal guests. His Eminence stands by the queen in a long taffeta robe, fire-colored, lined with ermine over a black skirt. His face is sad and stern. Is he thinking of père Joseph, so recently dead?

Has he spotted an uninvited guest? His gazing eye takes in all. Or is he simply fretted over the failure to appear of the duke of Weimar in whose honor he has written some verses to be sung? The king takes early leave, before the great curtains have parted again to reveal a splendid ballroom where the stage has just been. The cardinal bows to the queen, and she moves forward to the dais followed by her respectful host. Everyone knows that she fears and detests him, but on this occasion he might be a benevolent and protecting uncle. He has reached the pinnacle.

A court ball. (Bibliothèque Nationale, Paris. *Photo Giraudon*)

Above: Pope Urban VIII (Maffeo Barberini) by Bernini.
(Musée du Louvre, Paris. *Photo Giraudon*). *Below:*
Charles de Gonzague, duc de Nevers, later duke of
Mantua. *Right:* Chart showing French reconstitution of
the Valtelline. (*Photo Giraudon*)

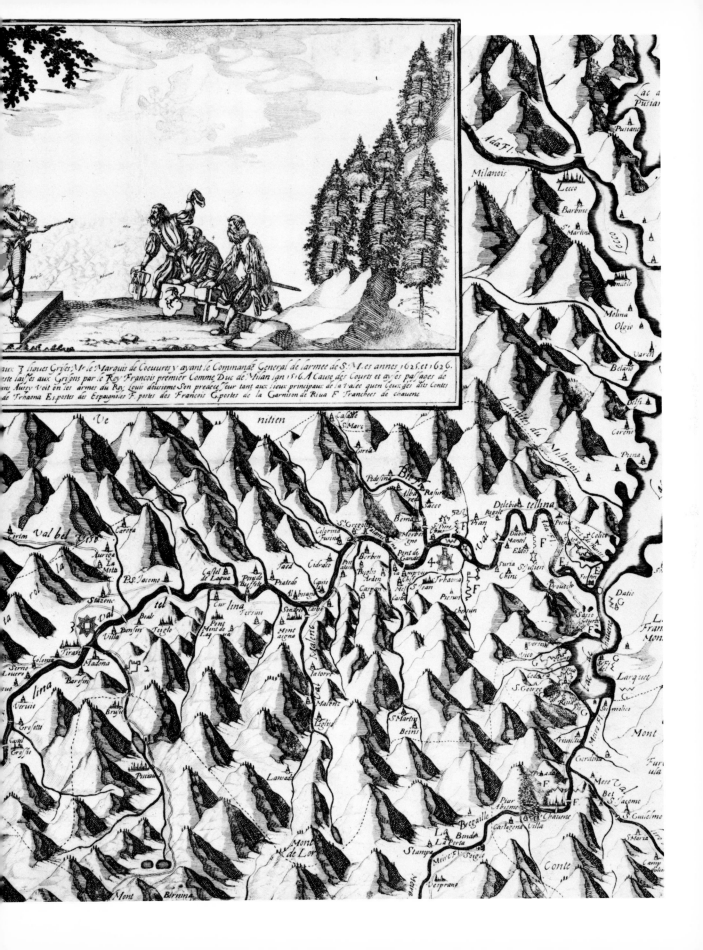

IX

Richelieu's Italian Policy (1624-1630)

I f you examine a map of France in 1624, you will see that she was almost entirely hemmed in by the Habsburg powers. The Spanish Netherlands, governed for Philip IV by his aunt, the archduchess Isabella, bordered on the north from Dunkerque to Verdun. Moving southeast and then south toward Geneva the border line passed the duchy of Lorraine, which owed fealty to the empire, and Franche-Comté, a Spanish principality. Then came the north Italian states, Savoy, Montferrat, and Genoa, heavily dominated, when not actually occupied, by Spain. All the way south, of course, Spain and France shared a border from the Atlantic to the Mediterranean. There was no clear egress except by sea, and there was almost no French navy.

What, it may be asked, did all this matter to a country that could supply its own needs by agriculture and manufacture? It mattered because of the constant terror of invasion. No French statesman could be absolutely sure that the emperor and the king of Spain might not one day be swayed to please God by uniting their dominions with France in a single German-Gallic-Hispanic Empire that would embrace all Catholic civilization and destroy heresy. Charlemagne, after all, had ruled such a world.

There were two obvious ways to avoid this threat. The first was to create a strong navy. The second was to extend the borders of France to impregnable areas wherever existing borders were incapable of being rendered impregnable.

Ultimately Richelieu and his successor, Mazarin, achieved these

Philip IV of Spain by Velázquez. (Courtesy The Frick Collection, New York)

aims. Artois, Verdun, and Metz in the north, Alsace and Bresse in the east, and Roussillon in the south were added permanently to France. A strong navy was built, and the nation would have been immune to the danger of invasion had not Louis XIV greedily exceeded the wisely restrained territorial ambitions of the two great cardinals and pushed his way into Germany, the Low Lands, and Spain, uniting all Europe against him under the generalship of Marlborough. One can be sure that Richelieu would have wept at the folly of the War of the Spanish Succession. But a monarchical system is only as strong as its silliest king. Louis XIV had nobody but himself to thank when he faced invasion as an old man and had to melt down his silver to pay the troops.

From the day he acquired power, Richelieu never relaxed his scrutiny of the Habsburg armor to watch for soft spots. Fortunately for him, there were many. The empire was embroiled in civil war, and the Dutch were in constant, vigorous revolt against a government in Madrid that seemed suicidally obsessed with their repression. Holland's galleys made it difficult for Spain to reinforce her troops in the Low Lands and to assist the emperor by sea, and she preferred to ship them to Genoa and thence north into Germany through the mountain passes. The best of these, the Valtelline, went through that part of Switzerland connecting the territory of the Milanese to the Austrian Tyrol. It was Richelieu's constant preoccupation to keep this pass under French control or at least neutral and so drive a wedge between the Habsburg allies.

When he became first minister in 1624, the forts in the Valtelline pass which had been taken from the Swiss by Spanish troops had been transferred to papal garrisons. Although Urban VIII, the Barberini pope, was ordinarily pro-French in his personal dispositions (he had never forgotten the delights of Paris which he had experienced as nuncio), the papal states were under the domination of Spain, which owned all of southern Italy and a good deal of the north, and papal control of the Valtelline was no guarantee that it would not be readily accessible for the passage of Spanish troops. Richelieu decided to occupy the Valtelline pass, and in a quick operation, taking only ninety days, he seized all but two of the forts. Urban VIII was indignant; Richelieu agreed to negotiate, and the Treaty of Monzon was signed. It was not wholly satisfactory to any of the parties. It stipulated that the forts should be restored and destroyed, but no provision was made that Spain should not use the pass in the future. Spain, in fact, continued not only to use it, but to claim that France, by the terms of the treaty, had waived all rights in it. At the time, however, the treaty was regarded as something of a triumph for Richelieu, for Spanish control of the Valtelline was temporarily suspended.

Five years later, in 1629, Vincenzo Gonzaga, duke of Mantua, died, leaving his double domain, Mantua and Montferrat, to his cousin, Charles de Gonzague, duc de Nevers, a subject of Louis XIII, who, like père Joseph, had long indulged in fantasies about launching a crusade to the Holy Land. Now he had to turn his energies, with French aid, to taking possession of his inheritance. Montferrat was a fief of the Holy Roman Empire, and the emperor summoned the Aulic Council to determine the validity of the will. The little principality was between Savoy and Milan, and its capital, Casale, commanded the route from Genoa to Milan, and thence to the Valtelline. The Spaniards, moving to forestall the claim of the French candidate, laid siege to Casale. Richelieu determined to intervene to support the Nevers claim and to raise the siege.

He had to wait until the fall of La Rochelle, but by January of 1629 he was ready to present his arguments for intervention in Italy to the king and the queen-mother. Marie de Médicis had begun now more openly to oppose her erstwhile favorite. She did not like the duc de Nevers, who had said that the Gonzagues had been royal while the Médicis were still in trade, and she did not like the increasingly apparent hostility of the cardinal's policy to her cousins in Madrid and Vienna. She was beginning to form a party that would always be for peace with the Habsburgs, and its two principal members were the Marillac brothers: Michel, the great lawyer and codifier, who was keeper of the seal, and Louis, his more dashing younger brother, who was one of the ablest of the marshals of France. However, Richelieu, with fresh laurels from La Rochelle, was able to prevail with Louis, who loved war, and he and the king now set off with the main army across the Alps to Casale.

The Horrors of War by Callot.

Israel ex. cum Priuil Reg.

Israel ex. Cum Priuilegio Regis.

Israel ex. Cum Priuil: Reg.

Left: The Suze Pass. (Bibliothèque Nationale, Paris. *Photo Documentation Française*). *Below:* Allegory of France triumphant under Louis XIII. (Bibliothèque Nationale, Paris. *Photo Bulloz*). *Opposite:* Defeat of the Spaniards and the siege of Arras. (*Photo Larousse*)

La defaicte des Espagnols a l'attaque du
Siege d'Arras l'Arriuee du Conuoy et la
Reddition de la ville d'Arras a l'obeissance du Roy

ARRAS

L'armee du Cal Infant

le Cl Gassion

la sortie des
espagnole hors dela ville

Fuitte des Espagnols

L'Arriuee du Connoy

M. du Hallier

le Mal
Chatillon

Duc de Chaulne

M. de la Mille
raye

la Valteline

Monsieur

M. de la Force

M. de
Rohan

M. de
Chatil
lon

Guienne

Poic
tou

Breta
gne

Norma
die

Pica
die

Tiera:
che

D. Charle

ge du Roy   S.P.Q.R.

I.D. Wtt

Suse, in Savoy, Spain's ally, lay in their way. The wily old duke sent his son, Victor Amadeus, who was married to Louis' sister Christine, to propose to the king that the town be swapped for a French one. Richelieu demanded sarcastically to know whether they wanted Orléans or Poitiers. The French then seized Suse, and Savoy came to terms. The Spaniards, uneasy without their ally, retreated from Casale. The first Italian expedition had had a rapid success, and the king went back to Paris. Richelieu returned by way of the south, through Languedoc, mopping up a few last Huguenot strongholds as he went.

The emperor, Ferdinand II, now moved to stir again the always-muddy waters of the north Italian situation. Angered by Nevers' refusal to acknowledge his right to determine the succession question, he sent an army of twenty thousand into Mantua which seized and largely destroyed that city. Spain, through her great general Spinola, whose handsome, aristocratic countenance is known to us from Velázquez' *Surrender of Breda*, resumed the siege of Casale. Savoy, as might have been expected, again came in with Spain. By the end of 1629 it was evident that all that had been accomplished in the first Italian expedition had been undone, and Richelieu embarked upon the second.

He led an army into Savoy and seized Pinerolo in the southwest. The duke of Savoy tried to cut his communications with France but was forestalled by Louis XIII himself at the head of a second army which seized Chambéry. These French successes were balanced by the arrival of the Imperial forces at Casale to join Spinola. But the hot summer brought a plague that caused a grim lull in the conflict. Its most distinguished victim was Spinola. Louis XIII and Richelieu withdrew to Lyon, where the king developed a dangerous fever.

Père Joseph in the meantime, as French ambassador, was attending a meeting of the Imperial diet in Regensburg. Among the matters on the agenda was the election of the emperor's son as king of the Romans with presumptive succession to the Imperial crown. Père Joseph opposed this—quite unnecessarily, as the Imperial succession in the Habsburg family was almost assured even without the Roman title—and while he labored the point, he was outplayed by the emperor's diplomats not only on the North Italian question but on the larger German question. The Treaty of Regensburg, in final form, provided that the Spaniards should withdraw from Casale, the Imperialists from Mantua, and the French from Italy except for Suse and Pinerolo. Furthermore, the French promised never to give aid to the enemies of the emperor. What would this have done to Richelieu's secret plans of encouraging dissent throughout Germany? Even the Nevers claim was not settled. It was left to the emperor.

Now came one of the great crises in Richelieu's life. The king had fallen desperately ill in Lyon. The queen, the queen-mother, and the leaders of the pro-Spanish party were with him. Weakened by illness and threatened with hell-fire if he continued to make war on the principal Catholic sovereigns, there was every likelihood that he would choose a peace ministry if he lived. And if he died, what hope for the cardinal would there be from King Gaston? Was it the moment to antagonize the king's enemies? Yet Richelieu did not hesitate. To the disgust of half of France and to the fury of the emperor, he publicly repudiated the treaty on the ground that père Joseph had exceeded his authority. The war went on; the king recovered and backed Richelieu. The latter had won his gamble.

He also won his war. Nevers became the duke of Mantua. The population of his new capital had been reduced by sack and plague to a quarter of its former size, but presumably omelettes were to be made only from broken eggs. The Treaty of Cherasco stipulated that all armies should withdraw from Mantua, and that the French should give up Suse and Pinerolo; but by a trick at the last moment Richelieu managed to hang on to Pinerolo. He had reason to be pleased with his policy. He had cut a gash in the belt that had been strangling France. Ultimately that gash was to be healed and the Valtelline restored to Spanish control, but by that time the Habsburg menace was in the past.

It was on the second Italian expedition that Richelieu met the man whom he would one day designate his successor. Giulio Mazarini, who dropped the final "i" when he became a French subject, was the soldier-diplomat who represented the pope. His social origin was obscure, but his charm and cleverness had brought him to high office. Richelieu had an immediate appreciation of his bargaining abilities, and decided that he was too good to be left to the Vatican. He easily prevailed upon him to come to France and change his citizenship. Later, he procured a cardinal's hat for him and bequeathed him to Louis XIII as first minister. Nothing more proves Louis' respect for Richelieu's opinion than his compliance with this dying instruction.

Cardinal Mazarin by Mignard. (Musée Condé, Chantilly. *Photo Giraudon*)

X

The Day of Dupes

Richelieu's decisiveness during the summer of 1630, when Louis XIII lay dangerously ill in Lyon, was typical of how he behaved (with one exception, during the siege of Corbie) at those times when his lifework was threatened. In such crises, compromise was impossible, because the game would not have been worth playing on compromised terms. He had bowed and scraped to achieve authority—yes. But only because he had a policy to save France. What sense would his life have made if he were to have achieved the authority only to scrap the policy? What would it gain a man to win the whole world and lose his soul?

There must have been moments when he could hardly understand how his opponents could fail to see anything so obvious. Was it not as clear as the nose on their face? France had to be strong, within and without. All Europe would then follow her lead—in arms, in art, in architecture, in poetry, in science. It was so obvious that even Marie de Médicis ought to have got the idea! Could she not understand that he *had* to use her, that it was her eternal glory to have been so used? Could she not see that she had a splendid future as the mother of the first monarch of Christendom? Richelieu's nervous twitches, his aches and his pains, his apprehensions and his fears, seem as petty as the jealousies of his enemies against the sweeping canvas of his political ideals. He was saying to the queen-mother and her party: "Look! This thing is bigger than you. Just give me time, and we'll all be great!"

The king had recovered and gone back to Paris, and Marie followed her son by barge down the Loire with the cardinal. They appeared to be getting on—he was all attention—but she had finally made up her mind that there was no future for her while he was in power, and she had resolved to force the issue as soon as she arrived at the capital. The date of her attempt was November 11, 1630, known in history as the "Day of Dupes."

Marie de Médicis.

There are different accounts of what actually happened, but there is essential agreement that the king called upon his mother at her Palais du Luxembourg and that Richelieu had the temerity to intrude upon their private interview by slipping in through a back door. "I'll wager that Your Majesties were speaking of me," he is reputed to have said. The queen-mother lost her head completely, and, according to most historians, railed like a fishwife, throwing her arms about and heaving her big bosom, while her son, humiliated, sat in moody silence and the cardinal, in tears, protested his loyalty. Whatever happened, it seems clear that Marie told the king that he had to choose between her and his minister and that when Louis left for his hunting lodge at Versailles, he had not made his decision. Word got around Paris that Marie had won, and the Luxembourg was thronged with a congratulating crowd. Michel de Marillac prepared himself for the portfolio of first minister.

It has become a historical tradition to see France here at the crossroads. Behind the vulgar, ranting queen lurked the forces of darkness: the bigotry of Catholic Spain and Austria which strove to thrust Europe back to pre-Reformation days; the power of restless, quarrelsome nobles who sought to preserve the heady joys of feudalism; the shallow philosophy that France was the property of a handful of peers and of priests who had no higher fealty than what they owed to Rome. Behind the weeping cardinal, on the other hand, was simply France, France as we conceive of her to this day, ordered, disciplined, beautiful—the nation where pleasure is an art and glory a duty.

Of course, the tradition may not be fair. Marie de Médicis, for all her Habsburg leanings, never recommended that France should bow to Vienna or Madrid. She merely sought alliance with fellow Catholic powers, an alliance that might have ended religious warfare in Europe. Would that have been so bad? To our disillusioned twentieth-century eyes was any Protestant faith worth the carnage of the Thirty Years' War? And, so far as Spanish hegemony in Europe was concerned, were not the Habsburg powers on the decline anyway? And, even with respect to internal dissensions, was not Michel de Marillac the author of the national code that Richelieu himself found it expedient to enforce? From such a point of view it could be argued that the cardinal in the first six years of his administration had already accomplished his two great objectives: the reduction of the power of the Huguenots and of the great nobles, and that France would have been better off had she been spared the efforts to which he devoted the next dozen in making war on the Habsburgs. The trouble with history is that one never knows what the alternative policy would have brought.

Richelieu seems to have agreed with the general opinion that the queen-mother had won. He was making plans to get away from Paris and the anticipated revenge of his enemies when the duc de Saint-Simon, a nonpolitical favorite of the king and father of the future memoirist, confided in him that Louis had not made up his mind and urged him strongly to wait. Richelieu did, and that night he was sent for to go to Versailles. His victory was complete. Louis, who wanted above all things to be a great king, must have seen vividly enough which of his two interlocutors at the Luxembourg was going to be the more helpful in achieving his goal. Marie had nothing to offer but her motherhood, and she had made a sorry hash of that.

She now announced grandly that she would never sit on the Council again while Richelieu was on it. Poor woman, what an idle threat! Then she managed to bring herself to grant an interview to the hated cardinal and to treat him with some degree of civility. But nothing, threats or good manners, was going to restore her influence at court. Michel de Marillac was ordered to give up his commission as keeper of the seal and retire to his country estate. Louis de Marillac, the marshal, was arrested at his headquarters in Italy. Gaston broke with the cardinal in January 1631 and went into open revolt. Marie decided that she had no hope but to join her younger son.

She had not at first meant to leave France. When she slipped away from Compiègne in July, she meant only to establish herself, independent of Louis and the cardinal, in the northern fortress of Lacapelle-Marival. But Richelieu, once again, was ahead of her. Warned of her plans, he had his own men at Lacapelle-Marival, and its gates were closed to her. There was nothing for Marie to do but go on, and "on" took her over the border into self-imposed exile in the Spanish Netherlands. She had framed herself as a traitor and could not now return without crawling before her former protégé. This was perhaps the only humiliation that she was to be spared in her next dozen years of wandering and begging. She did not set foot again on French soil. Of course, she could not have played more perfectly into Richelieu's hand. Even her dying would have been less advantageous; it might have aroused the king's remorse. She had the consideration to postpone this event until six months before Richelieu's own.

If the cardinal had proof of a general conspiracy amounting to treason between the queen-mother and her party, he did not see fit to offer it. Gaston, of course, was an obvious rebel, but what about Louis de Marillac? Nothing was ever proved against him but some minor peculation in army supplies, a custom almost a perquisite of all general officers of the time. Yet Richelieu appointed a special commission of judges, selected by himself, to try him for this as a capital offense and had them meet at his own château of Rueil! And when the death sentence had been obtained by a bare majority of even that star chamber, the victim was rushed on the same day to his decapitation in the Place de Grève.

Why? Richelieu glosses over it in his memoirs, yet one never feels that he was ashamed. Some things may have been difficult for him to explain to others; one doubts that he ever found difficulty in explaining them to himself. When he wanted a man's head, as he wanted Marillac's, and as he was later to want Urbain Grandier's and François de Thou's, he was willing to stretch the law to a farce to get it. In the case of Marillac personal vindictiveness was a possible motive, for Marillac had probably planned the same fate for Richelieu, but it could hardly have been so in the case of the other two. One surmises that the cardinal believed that he had some kind of public obligation, at whatever cost to fair judicial procedure, to make an example of Marillac. Marie de Médicis had gone over to Spain; Gaston and the duc de Montmorency, one of the greatest nobles of the realm, were in armed rebellion. It was time to throw in their teeth the head of a marshal of France who had been, even legally, of their persuasion. What shocks us most today is that a deeply educated man and churchman, a student of government, and a sophisticated observer of his fellow men, could have believed so absolutely, so unquestioningly, not in the doctrine that the ends justified the means, but that *his* ends justified *his* means. Richelieu's faith in the validity of his policies would have seemed like fanaticism in a man less coldly rational.

He did not, as it turned out, need the execution of Marillac, at least so far as Gaston was concerned. The rebellion was a fizzle from the start. Louis de Marillac perished on the scaffold on May 10, 1632. His brother Michel died, of natural causes, in August. The duc de Montmorency was wounded and captured on September 1, and executed at Toulouse on October 30. Gaston made his usual cringing submission and went unscathed.

Much more has been written about Montmorency's trial than Marillac's. He was gallant, charming, beloved, a fine flower of chivalry. But the general indignation at his death was the sheerest sentimentality. What had he cared about the poor troops who perished in his ridiculous rebellion? He was a rebel, and rebels must prevail or die. The rule is the same today as it was then. "When treason prospers, none dare call it treason." But Montmorency did not prosper. He bequeathed to the first minister the famous slaves of Michelangelo, which the cardinal put up in the courtyard of his château at Richelieu.

The casualty of the Day of Dupes for whom one feels the greatest sympathy is the charming Bassompierre. He was imprisoned in the Bastille until the cardinal's death eleven years later. It was said that, in a council of the queen-mother's friends assembled to debate what should be the fate of Richelieu if they prevailed, Marillac had opted for death, Guise for exile, and Bassompierre for imprisonment, and that each was given his own sentence by the triumphant cardinal.

Bassompierre's account of his arrest and imprisonment is touching. He starts the account:

> The next day, Monday, the 24th of February, I rose before daybreak and burned more than six thousand love letters that I had received from various ladies, fearing that if I was taken to prison they might come and search my house and find something which would be harmful, these being the only papers in my possession which could harm anybody.

Warned by friends that he was surely going to be arrested and should therefore escape (a fairly routine, indeed an expected procedure where the authorities did not wish the death of the person appre-

Henri II, duc de Montmorency. He personified the age of chivalry and the ideal of *noblesse oblige*. But to him all of this was perfectly consistent with armed rebellion against the crown. (Musée du Louvre, Paris. *Photo Giraudon*)

Above left: Louis de Marillac, comte de Beaumont and marshal of France. *Above right:* Michel de Marillac, author of *Le Code Michau.* (*Photos Richard Kalvar/VIVA*). *Below:* Marie de Médicis' Palais du Luxembourg, a proper residence for the mother of France and the mother-in-law of Spain and England. (Bibliothèque Nationale, Paris. *Photo Larousse*)

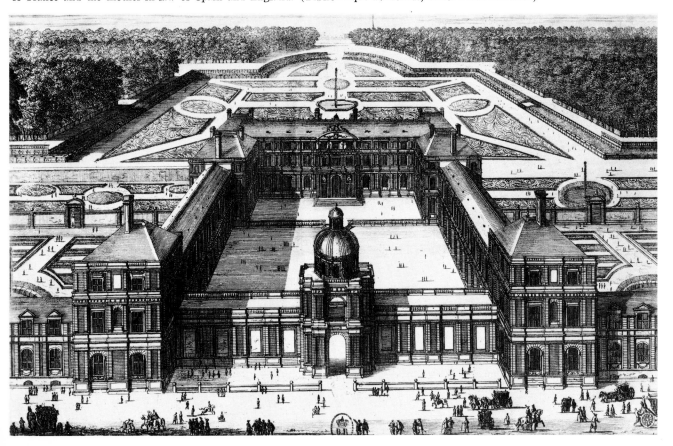

hended), he nonetheless refused and went off that morning to the court at Senlis. He found the king in the queen's reception chamber. Louis came up to him and said encouragingly: "Here is good company," and then spoke of Bassompierre's difficulties respecting his mother and the cardinal. Bassompierre went straight to the point and told the king that he had been warned that he would be arrested and had, therefore, presented himself at court so that His Majesty should not have the trouble of looking for him. The king protested: "How could you have thought that I would do anything like that? You know how fond I am of you." At this word was brought to the king that the cardinal was waiting in the king's reception chamber, and Louis took leave of the company, warning Bassompierre to be at Senlis the next morning early to march the guards to Paris. But later that morning, when the king returned from his visit to the cardinal to play his guitar, he avoided Bassompierre's glance and never said a word to him.

The next morning, when Bassompierre awoke at his house in Paris, Monsieur de Launay, lieutenant of the Royal Bodyguards, entered his room and said: "Sir, with tears in my eyes and a bleeding heart, I, who for twenty years have been your faithful soldier, am obliged to tell you that the king has given orders for your arrest." And so Bassompierre began his long term at the Bastille. Although the cardinal twice wrote him polite letters asking for the loan of one of his châteaux near the northern front, he would never agree to release him. He and his royal master were at their most congenial in questions of discipline.

Louis XIII with his brother Gaston, duc d'Orléans. (*Photo Petit-Documentation Française*)

Marie de Médicis and her court entering the Spanish Netherlands. (Bibliothèque Nationale, Paris. *Photo Lauros-Giraudon*)

XI

Lion of the North

The Emperor Ferdinand II was a bigot on a gargantuan scale. At his door, a large portion of the atrocities of the Thirty Years' War may be laid. When he was elected to the Imperial crown, he vowed to restore the Roman Catholic faith throughout the empire and made a pilgrimage to the Italian village of Loreto to which the Virgin's house had been miraculously transported from the Holy Land. Throughout his reign he was the slave of strict dogmatists. He once consulted a commission of twenty-four priests as to the propriety of signing a treaty with a Protestant sovereign. His son, the future Ferdinand III, used to pray in his tent before an image of the Virgin while his troops were engaged in battle. It was to such men that the fate of millions was committed in the seventeenth century. Yet had Ferdinand II not been so adamant on the question of the restoration of all Catholic church lands, no matter how anciently expropriated, he might have succeeded in his ultimate purpose. Essentially, he defeated himself.

By the end of 1630 his troops, together with those of the League of German Catholic Princes, commanded by Tilly, the elector of Bavaria's brilliant but savage general, had defeated Christian IV of Denmark and controlled central Europe from the Adriatic to the Baltic. Richelieu's efforts to detach Bavaria from the League had been

Gustavus Adolphus, King of Sweden. (Pinakothek, Munich. *Photo Haufstaenfl-Giraudon*)

totally unavailing. Imperialism stood at a height that it would never reach again. It was high time for the cardinal to bring the king of Sweden into the German mess.

He might have come anyway. Gustavus Adolphus had no wish for a united Catholic empire on the Baltic, and he fancied the idea of appearing as a *deus ex machina* from the north to rally the drooping Protestant cause. But war was expensive, even when troops lived largely on conquest, and Swedish funds were low. It was Hercule de Charnacé who, during the siege of La Rochelle, first discussed with Richelieu the possibility of using Sweden to deepen the embroilment of Germany. He was known to père Joseph, whose romantic notions of crusading in the Middle East he shared. Richelieu was expert at turning this kind of zeal to his own practical purposes. How he was able so successfully to persuade these intense Catholics—who were also brilliant men—that the cause of the Church was best served by pouring millions into the hands of Protestant mercenaries must remain a mystery, but there is no question that he did. The Catholic cause in the minds of Charnacé and père Joseph became completely identified with the political hegemony of France. The former was dispatched to Gustavus Adolphus, and the acting French ambassador, a traitor in Gaston's pay, was kidnaped, returned to France, and decapitated.

The Lion of the North was not an easy man to deal with. He was quick to resent the notion that he might be the mercenary of France or even that his proposed invasion of Germany had anything to do with French assistance. Perhaps it did not. But he certainly needed the money. He embarrassed Charnacé by insisting on the restoration of Frederick V to the Palatinate, then held by the Elector Maximilian of Bavaria whose potential leadership of a third party in Germany was Richelieu's constant pipe dream. An agreement was finally struck which stipulated that Sweden would maintain thirty thousand foot soldiers and six thousand horse in Germany, and guarantee freedom of worship for Catholics in territory which they occupied (the usual pious provision necessitated by Richelieu's churchly rank). France, in return, would pay Sweden an annual subsidy of four hundred thousand thalers. The question of the Palatinate was left moot.

Gustavus Adolphus now landed at Stettin and proceeded south to Frankfurt an der Oder. At Breitenfeld, near Leipzig, he astonished Europe by winning the greatest battle of the Thirty Years' War, and the empire suddenly fell open before him. He could have gone east to Vienna and proclaimed himself emperor. Instead, he chose to march through southern Germany to the Rhine. He had further victories at Erfurt, at Frankfurt am Main, at Mainz. He then turned southeast into Bavaria and lodged himself in Maximilian's own palace at Nuremberg, surrounded by the treasures of the elector's collection. Small wonder that in Rome and Madrid he was regarded as a new Attila.

Richelieu, too, was appalled. Had he substituted for a bad neighbor a worse? The one consistent aspect of his foreign policy had been to spread dissension around France in order to reduce the dangers of invasion. He did not want the Thirty Years' War to end in a decisive victory either for the Swedish king or for the Protestant princes or for the Catholic League or for the emperor. The Treaty of Westphalia, signed six years after his death, was very much what he had worked for. It kept Germany divided and relatively powerless for another century. The same policy was employed in Spain, where he supported the rebels in Portugal and Catalonia, and in northern Italy, where he supported Mantua.

What of the moral aspect of such a policy? Not all the millions of deaths in the carnage of the era can be blamed on the cardinal, but neither can it be denied that he poured as much oil on the flames as he could and borrowed more when his supply ran short. If one had lived in Mantua, sacked by Imperialist troops, or in Catalonia, racked and tortured by a revengeful Philip IV, or anywhere in Germany, where life became as frightful as history has ever recorded, one would indeed have cursed the man in the red robe in Paris, who burned his candles late poring over a map of Europe to see where he could raise more hell. Yet Richelieu could have justly stated that his own territorial ambitions were modest, that he took less than he could have taken, that he wanted only a safe France in which to cultivate peacefully the Gallic genius. Was it *his* fault that his neighbors chose to engage in ridiculous religious wars? And could anyone deny that the Habsburgs dreamed of ruling the world? Was it not only common sense to hamper them wherever they could be hampered? And was it not his plain duty to his king to accomplish this, wherever possible, with French gold rather than French lives?

If we grant him his premise, perhaps we must absolve him. Certainly in our day morality would have justified the support of even the bloodiest revolt against Hitler. If Philip IV and Ferdinand II had really been united in a common purpose to humble and dominate France, the cardinal's implacable policy of retaliation might have been proper. But were they? Charles V, who had ruled all the territories of both, had split up his empire because it had proven impossible to govern efficiently as a unit. The Habsburg cousins were by no means always agreed, and their power and authority were already in the grip of decay. Spain, a frozen bureaucracy, way behind the times, and ever-dependent on gold from the New World, would be a third-rate European power in another generation. The Holy Roman Empire, divided into dozens of semiautonomous states and plagued with religious hate, would in the same period become an empty form. Did Richelieu have to do anything but wait?

But how was he to know that? How, for that matter, do we? That is the bafflement of history—one never knows. Perhaps it was Richelieu's policy that brought about the decline of Spain and of the historic role of the emperor. Perhaps without it they would have regained their old eminence. Perhaps. Yet the twentieth century has taught us certain lessons. We have learned that the development of a nation's power may not necessarily depend on the outcome of the wars in which it engages. Consider the victories of England in 1918 and 1945. Consider the defeats of Germany in the same years and of Russia in 1905 and 1917. Consider the defeat of Japan in 1945. It is not merely a joke that one cannot today afford to win a war. For generations historians have argued backward from the rise of French power to attribute it to Richelieu. Now we can see that it may have been coming anyway, or even that he may have hindered it. For we have also learned that an aggressive defense can create the very offense that it is designed to frustrate. D. P. O'Connell, who has written the deepest and most documented study of Richelieu in recent years, who has examined all of the treaties that he negotiated, permits himself to speculate that the cardinal may have actually brought into being the very Habsburg solidarity that was his lifetime bogey. He may have been a kind of seventeenth-century John Foster Dulles, dangerously exasperating the enemy that he was seeking to contain. Certainly it is true that Olivares, his opposite number in Madrid, cried angrily that everywhere he turned the cardinal blocked him!

But even if all this were so, could Richelieu have foreseen it? Possibly. The peace party in France constantly argued that an alliance with Spain would be more fruitful than a war. Richelieu identified them with the exiled queen-mother and with treason, but their arguments may still have been reasonable. Why should a predominantly Catholic France have feared a predominantly Catholic Germany? Did not the continuance of religious strife constantly stir up the Huguenots at home? Would not a France strong at home have been able to repel any invader? Was she strengthened by the peasant revolts brought on by the terrible costs of the war with Spain? Between the declaration of this war in 1635 and the cardinal's death seven years later there were no less than forty local insurrections in towns all over France. Considering how grim were the reprisals, the condition of the peasants must have been dire indeed. The real fortresses in France might not have been necessarily the border towns, whose occupation and reinforcement so obsessed the first minister, but the big interior cities. A France at peace and prosperous might have been impregnable. Think what thirty years of peace did for England under Elizabeth. Surely more than all the wars of Henry VIII.

Ferdinand II, desperate at the Swedish onslaught, had now to recall Wallenstein, the bombastic general whose overweening ambition had necessitated his retirement, and grant him all his demands, including the right to negotiate a peace, in order to induce him to fight the invader. The two greatest military figures of the age met at Lützen in Saxony. The dark deity that watched over the cardinal removed Gustavus Adolphus from the picture just as he had fulfilled his role, just, indeed, as he was beginning to overdo it. The battle may have been technically a victory for the Swedes, but the death of Gustavus, whose stripped corpse was hardly recognizable, more than compensated the Imperialists. Richelieu immediately found it easier to bargain with the more tractable Swedes, who had now lost their momentum. From 1632, the year of the battle, to 1634, the year of the Battle of Nordlingen, the cardinal was able to contemplate a very satisfactory stalemate and to negotiate with everybody in sight. Even Wallenstein sent overtures to him, offering to desert at a price and bring his army over to the Protestant cause. Oxenstierna, the Swedish chancellor, was not keen on this, knowing that Wallenstein, once victorious, would try to kick the Swedes out of Germany, but Richelieu was delighted, in the words of his biographer Carl J. Burckhardt, "not only because of the check which such a rebellion would offer the House of Austria, but because of the disorders which could not fail to attend it." For once, Louis XIII thought his minister had gone too far. When Ferdinand II got wind of his general's treachery and had him murdered, Louis announced publicly that he hoped all who betrayed their sovereigns would end so. Richelieu, informed of this, was upset and expressed his dismay that the king should have made the statement. But Louis, from time to time, liked to remind his principal servant that he was still a servant.

The Battle of Nordlingen, in Bavaria, broke the power of the Swedes and Protestants, and once again the Imperialist cause prevailed. What had Richelieu's policy now availed? He had sacrificed the lives of thousands of Mantuans, and spent vast sums to block the path of the Spaniards through north Italy to Germany. Yet the cardinal-infante, Philip IV's military brother, was able to march an army of twenty thousand men from Italy to meet on the Danube an Imperial army commanded by the emperor's son. Richelieu had brought Gustavus into Sweden, and the Swedes were now defeated. For all the cardinal's successes in northern Italy, for all the carnage he had created in Germany, for all the mincemeat he had made of the emperor's plans for a universal church, he still looked across the Rhine at a hostile, united Spanish and Imperial army under a brilliant general. Had he, as O'Connell speculates, created it?

Emperor Ferdinand II. (Bibliothèque Nationale, Paris. *Photo Larousse*)

It was now at last that he abandoned his indirection and resorted to open hostilities. Using the excuse of the Spanish occupation of Trèves, a French ally, he declared war on Philip IV. A herald was dispatched to announce the declaration to the cardinal-infante in Brussels in the old formal medieval way, but nobody would receive him. As the poor man rode disconsolately off in his splendid uniform he saw some ladies in a coach laughing at him. It was the exiled Marie de Médicis and her ladies.

Acrostic sonnet in honor of Marie de Médicis.

XII

Urbain Grandier

Aldous Huxley has told the terrible story of the devils of Loudun too vividly to have it repeated here. All we need be concerned with is why the cardinal and père Joseph interested themselves so directly in procuring the condemnation of the priest Urbain Grandier for witchcraft.

A group of Ursuline nuns in Loudun were seized with a kind of corporate frenzy in which they behaved and spoke in a most violent and lewd manner. In their maudlin ravings they identified Urbain Grandier as the source of their bewitchment. Grandier had antagonized a number of important persons in the town by his arrogance. He kept a mistress. He had written a tract in favor of the marriage of priests. He had opposed, as an early lover of landmarks, the destruction of the fortifications of Loudun. When his enemies united to use the testimony of the nuns against him, he was doomed. Richelieu's "butcher," the intendant Laubardemont, was sent down to conduct the trial, and the wretched Grandier was burned alive after the most frightful tortures.

Various theories have been introduced to explain Richelieu's interest in the matter. One of the Ursuline nuns was a distant cousin of his. Grandier had taken precedence over Richelieu in a church ceremonial, way back in the days when the latter was bishop of Luçon, which is near Loudun. Richelieu resented the priest's meddling in the fortification matter. But all of these reasons seem too petty. The cardinal was not a vindictive man. He was merciless, as we have seen, but only where something vital was at stake. And that vital something was almost always a question of law and order. Perhaps that is the clue.

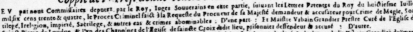

Execution of Urbain Grandier. The wretched man was seated because his legs had been broken on the wheel.

It must be remembered that the Loudun scandal had spread all over France. What could be more disorderly than a group of Ursuline nuns, including some of noble birth, including, worst of all, a cousin of the founder of all order, rolling about the floor and shrieking the most appalling obscenities under the claim that they were bewitched by Satan? Did it not discredit the church and its priests? Was it not just the kind of sordid episode that a cardinal-first minister intent on obtaining absolute authority would find most objectionable? Richelieu was always expedient when it came to sacrificing the individual to the cause. The way these things were usually handled was by torturing and burning the accused witch. Well then, he may have directed, let "justice" go forward and let the matter be ended as soon as possible.

It is perfectly possible that Richelieu believed in witches, at least at times. He certainly implied that he did so in his memoirs. But then, of course, it would have hardly looked well to have allowed a man to be burned alive for a crime in which the fountain of justice did not believe. The cardinal may have reasoned with himself: The man Grandier has brought great scandal on the Church by the seduction of respectable women in Loudun. He has fathered at least one bastard. He is known for his lax views on priestly celibacy. Might not the image of such a man have aroused disordered sexual thoughts in the minds of cloistered women and brought about the convulsions at the Ursuline priory? Is he not therefore guilty as charged—whether directly, through Satan, or, more subtly, through the example of his own dissolute life? After such a deliberation, Richelieu would not have hesitated to let the law take its normal, terrible course.

The most chilling aspect of the case is the hallucination that it offers: a twentieth-century man being tried in the seventeenth century. Grandier was modern in his cynicism and in the candid indulging of his appetites. His essay on celibacy and the priesthood makes an interesting distinction between the passionate oath of the monk who embraces chastity for the love of chastity and the more formal oath of the priest who submits to chastity because it is a requirement of office. Grandier behaved in all respects like a totally reasonable man, except that he was impolitic in underestimating the forces of bigotry and superstition that surrounded him, and the vileness of people who would use such forces to put him out of the way. At his trial he became a hero—at least to us. His refusal to admit his guilt under torture was splendid if futile. If we try Richelieu's other victims by the standards of their century, we cannot help trying Grandier by our own.

Reading Huxley's ghastly inventory of the torments inflicted on the alleged witch, one wonders if Richelieu's whole game was worth the candle. Was his sacred principle of centralization worth the agony of that unjustly condemned man? Consider what was done to Grandier and then look ahead to the end results of the cardinal's policies and envision the pompous, ridiculous court of Louis XIV with all its red heels, its simpering, its bloody, pointless wars. Might it not have been just as well to leave things as they were? Yet history is very often a choice of repellent alternatives. Had France been left a prey to the death struggles of its decayed feudalism, the horrors of the Thirty Years' War might have been perpetrated within its borders and a much larger number of Grandiers might have been broken on the wheel. It is necessary to remember Michelet's estimate that a million people were executed for witchcraft in Europe during the seventeenth century. The France that grew out of Richelieu's plans was a centralized, homogeneous, and cultivated nation. Louis XIV, for all his crimes against liberty and the dignity of man's soul, was at least able to abolish the death penalty for witchcraft and, thanks to Richelieu's centralizing policy, to enforce his edict throughout the nation. Seen from this point of view, Grandier may not have died totally in vain.

XIII

Richelieu and Corneille

As Richelieu professed himself a great lover of literature and even claimed that he was at his happiest composing verses, it may be profitable to examine the story of his relations with Pierre Corneille. Corneille is supposed to have said that he owed the cardinal too much to speak against him but had suffered too much at his hands to speak for him. Yet a legend exists that when the poet's future father-in-law objected to Corneille's suit, Richelieu summoned the former to the Palais-Cardinal and persuaded him to consent. And it is certainly true that Corneille went as far as even the most menial flatterer of that flattering day could go in his dedication of *Horace*:

> Watching Your Eminence's expression on the occasions when we poets have had the honor to read aloud to him has been a unique opportunity to learn the merit of our own work. By taking note of what Your Eminence approves and disapproves we can tell what in our work is good and what bad. . . . I have gained more instruction in two hours at such readings than I would have in ten years alone with my books.

Really! Is there anything more unattractive than a surly curmudgeon, bristling with prickly pride and vaunted independence, who is at the same time a toady? Corneille as a human being was perfectly impossible—like many of the world's greatest artists. He could never forgive the cardinal for the Academy's judgment of *Le Cid*.

What happened? In 1637, Corneille, at the age of only thirty-one, produced *Le Cid*, which was an immediate hit. It had something for everybody: action and romance for the pit, beautiful verses for the

P. CORNEILLE. 1647.

Pierre Corneille. (Musée de Versailles. *Photo Bulloz*)

intellectuals, and a fiery, passionate pace for both. Yet to the more classically minded of Corneille's fellow playwrights the piece was anathema. It conformed only superficially to the unities of space, time, and action. It was less like a tragedy of the period than like a drama of Victor Hugo, all noise and color, of two hundred years later. It is not surprising that the academic community found it necessary to attack this glittering snake in their garden of ordered dullness.

Corneille handled his defense badly. The political sense that had prompted him to dedicate his tragedy to the cardinal's niece, Madame de Combalet, deserted him at the first sign of opposition. He answered his critics with an explosion of self-adulation. In the poem "Excuse à Ariste" he explored the magnitude of his own merit and urged it as an excuse for the magnitude of his self-satisfaction. "Who knows our own worth more truly than we ourselves?" he demanded. This aroused wide mockery and indignation. It is bad enough for writers to have to recognize a superior; it is unbearable for them when the latter throws his superiority in their faces. Boisrobert, the poetaster who played the precarious role in the cardinal's household of self-appointed jester, going from one daring liberty to another and counting on a final explosive, hysteria-creating joke to save him from the Bastille, put on a parody of Le Cid, possibly before Richelieu himself. The scholarly world laughed, but no doubt those laughs were sour enough.

Much more serious for Corneille was the suggestion of the playwright Scudéry that the French Academy, newly instituted by the cardinal, should judge the question of whether or not Le Cid conformed to the canons of taste. Richelieu approved the suggestion, and the Academy duly rendered its ridiculous judgment that Le Cid violated the classic unities and used words inappropriate for tragic drama. The ruling did not have the effect of law. Corneille was not obliged to alter his style. But the expression of so high a literary authority, backed by a political one, was not, in that century, to be lightly ignored. Corneille was crushed.

There has been much speculation among historians as to why Richelieu, who liked Corneille's plays enough to grant him a pension and to arrange his marriage, should have lowered himself to assist a cabal to discredit his protégé's masterpiece. A common opinion has been that the cardinal, a would-be tragedian himself, was jealous of Corneille's literary merit, but there is no evidence elsewhere in Richelieu's record of any such extraordinary pettiness of character. A more plausible theory is that the cardinal, a declared enemy of duelists, disliked the fight in the play between the hero and the heroine's father. Another is that he may have feared the effect on the public, at a critical period in the war with Spain, of a popular play with a Spanish warrior for hero. But the trouble with both of these theories is that the judgment of the Academy came *after* the production. If Richelieu had considered the play dangerous propaganda either for duels or for Spain, he could have prevented its production altogether. It would not have been like him to go about the business in so devious and ineffective a way.

It seems more likely that the reasons for the cardinal's opposition were purely literary. His literary principles were at one with all his others. They centered around his preoccupation with orderliness. The formality of classical rules, even when they verged on the pedantic, was balm to a soul that so abhorred untidiness. And *Le Cid*, as swashbuckling as a Verdi opera, must have struck him as very untidy indeed. Besides, had it not given rise to an unseemly literary row, with all the first poets of what the cardinal liked to conceive of as a new Augustan era vilifying each other disgustingly in the public prints? Was this not precisely the kind of crisis that he had created the Academy to cope with? Should peace and purpose not reign in letters as they now reigned in France?

The same first minister who had quelled La Rochelle and bade the Protestants to live in harmony with the rest of France now ordered Corneille to cease his pamphleteering. Corneille, furious, lapsed into a grumpy silence that lasted for four years. But the cardinal in the end, as usual, got his way. When Corneille emerged from his sulks, he decided that the best way to defeat his opponents was at their own game. His next play, *Horace*, a masterpiece which confounded his critics, conformed strictly to the classic unities and was dedicated to the cardinal.

Richelieu's victory, however, was Pyrrhic. If Corneille became the greatest spokesman of the cardinal's conception of *"gloire,"* if he rose to express in verse the sublimity of the cardinal's political and military ambition for France, an ambition that culminated in the age of Louis XIV, he also expressed the chaos and sterility to which the same age ultimately pointed. Corneille was a wonderfully honest poet. It is the rugged integrity of his sullen soul that gives a craggy magnificence even to his later tragedies, generally considered unreadable by all but the blindest French admirers. He had the passionate devotion to soldiers and kings that was found in so many burghers of his day, but this admiration was always accompanied by a burgher's vision of the cost of military and royal games. Corneille loved the paths of glory while perfectly understanding that they led only to the grave.

Three of his plays, one early, one middle, and one late, illustrate the development in his work, from birth, through splendor, to dissolution, of Richelieu's concept of *gloire.*

We see its origin in an early comedy—of very few laughs and those very wry ones—called *La Place Royale.* The hero, or what we today should be tempted to call the anti-hero, Alidor, is an interesting forerunner of Alceste in Molière's *Le Misanthrope.* He is in love with a beautiful and charming young woman, Angélique, who is equally in love with him and who, furthermore, is rich and of good family. But so easy a situation is not for Alidor. He points out to his friend, Cléandre, that as long as love holds him in its sway, he cannot call himself a free man—he has ceased to be in charge of his destiny. He then proceeds, like a modern existentialist, to regain command of his life by deliberately insulting his beloved and by telling her that he prefers another. When in natural fury she turns to another suitor, he makes plans to abduct her in order that he may give her to his friend, Cléandre, and so reduce his own jealousy. Foiled in this endeavor, he decides at last to give in to his passion and to marry Angélique, but it is too late. In disgust, she has decided to enter a convent, and at the final curtain we see Alidor tickled pink to find his problem solved in such a way that he can be rid of his sweetheart without giving her to another! He is uniformly despicable throughout the play, unlike Molière's melancholy Alceste, for whom we have a reluctant admiration. Alceste, after all, is unable to live in the world because he is unable to make the shabby compromises that we all make. But Alidor's love of his own liberty of action is a thing which ultimately negates everything that is worthwhile in life. For an Alidor can never, like Alceste, be content to be a recluse. To prove to himself that he has freedom of action, he must be constantly imposing his will on others, and to make such megalomania attractive, another name must be found for it. So *gloire* is born.

In his greatest tragedy, *Horace*, Corneille lays these cards even more clearly on the table. The rival cities, Rome and Albe, have decided to settle their differences through the battle of three champions selected by each side. Horace and his two brothers are selected by Rome, Curiace and his two brothers by Albe. Horace is married to Sabine, a sister of Curiace, and Curiace is engaged to Horace's sister, Camille. Corneille leans over backward to make it entirely clear to his audience that the defeated party is not to regard itself as in any way humiliated. The citizens of the losing city will become subjects, not slaves: they will be "without shame, without tribute and without other bondage than that of following the flags of the victor." The two cities will thereafter form a single empire. But to Horace, death is still preferable to defeat. For his ambition, there is no possible place but the top one. The mere suggestion that such a philosophy may be flawed arouses his violent temper, and when his sister, distracted on hearing of her lover's death, curses Rome, he slaughters her without a scruple. Corneille seems to concede that Horace may have gone a bit far here, but there appears to be no question in his mind that Horace's father who condones the deed and the king of Rome who pardons it are acting not only wisely but justly. Horace is a totally Nazi hero in a totally Nazi play, if one can admit that nobility of thought and language are consistent with such a description. Why not? They are in Wagner's *Ring*.

Corneille, however, was too honest to leave the matter there. He had later to push on and to show where *gloire* ultimately leads. In one of his final tragedies, *Attila*, we see the Roman Empire, founded by such heroes as Horace centuries before, in the clutch of a bloody and merciless dictator who travels about Italy with an entourage in which

183

EMINENTISSIMO PRINCIPI
CARDINALI DVCI DE RICHELIEV.

Opposite above: Setting for *Mirame*, a play by Desmarets on which Riche-
lieu was supposed to have collaborated. (Bibliothèque Nationale, Paris.
Photo Larousse). *Opposite below:* Richelieu at the Sorbonne. He is buried
in the chapel seen at the back. (Bibliothèque Nationale, Paris. *Photo
Lauros-Giraudon*) *Above:* A theater, 1630. (Bibliothèque Nationale, Paris.
Photo Larousse)

Mon superbe Logis, est vne prison forte,
Les quatre murs me seruent de Dames & valets,
Je n'attends que ce iour, (mes amis) que ie sorte,
Et qu'vn cruel bourreau termine mes regrets.

Léonora Galigaï in prison. (Bibliothèque Nationale, Paris. *Photo Giraudon*)

captive kings are reduced to the role of courtiers. It is true that there are references in the play to the enlightened king of the Gauls, an off-stage parallel to Louis XIV, and we hear of how happy people are under his beneficent despotism, but it is on Attila that the spotlight rests, and it is Attila who shows us what absolute monarchy comes to.

Like Alidor, Attila resents his own passion for Ildione. Attila must rule the world—and himself. He is the supreme, the ultimate expression of the Corneille hero, always the happy object of the world's hate, faithful to his own deposit of tyrannical power, the terror of all, the scourge of God. Nobody can stop him. No power on earth can arrest his bloody course but the eruption of his own blood. It is a nosebleed that finally carries him off and resolves the action of the play! Would any other playwright have been *that* faithful to history? Would Racine? The great dark hero, the equal of God, the reverse of God, is the end of the road for *gloire.*

Had Richelieu been a poet, he might have seen it this way, too. But that was the very last thing that he was, for all his professed pleasure in writing verses and for all his supposed co-authorship with Desmarets of that mildest of tragedies, *Mirame.* It was as a writer of prose that he professed the sentiments of Attila:

> All politicians agree that when the people are too comfortable
> it is impossible to keep them within the bounds of their duty.
> They must be compared to mules, which being used to burdens,
> are spoiled more by rest than by labor.

The remarkable thing about this quotation is not that he should have thought it but that he should have written it. Yet in fairness to Richelieu we should not leave the topic of his relation to literature without pointing out that if his contributions to tragic drama as a critic and poet were slight, his contributions to prose show a strength and firmness of style that might have made him, had he had the time and inclination, a minor Saint-Simon.

The vast memoirs under his name that cover the reign of Louis XIII are probably largely the work of secretaries, but some of the entries of memorable events have a ring that could have come from no voice but his. Here, for example, is his comment on the death of the unhappy maréchale d'Ancre, Concini's wife, executed as a witch after the assassination of her husband:

> Coming out of prison and seeing the great multitude of people who had gathered to watch her, she exclaimed: "How many people have gathered to see one poor wretch go by!" Her humility before God made her also humble before men. His grace in her brought about a great change in those who watched. They became different people; their eyes were drenched with pity.

And here is his comment on the death of Gustavus Adolphus at Lützen at the very peak of his dazzling military career:

> The death of the king of Sweden is a great example of the frailty of man. All the lands that he had wrested from his neighbors, all the riches that he had seized in Germany, did not suffice, when he yielded up his soul, to make up so much as a shirt to cover his nakedness. High as his birth and glory had carried him, he was now prostrate on the earth, trampled on by the horses of friend and foe alike. He was a corpse like the humblest—torn, bloody, unrecognizable. Even his intimates could hardly identify him. Such was the end of his splendor.

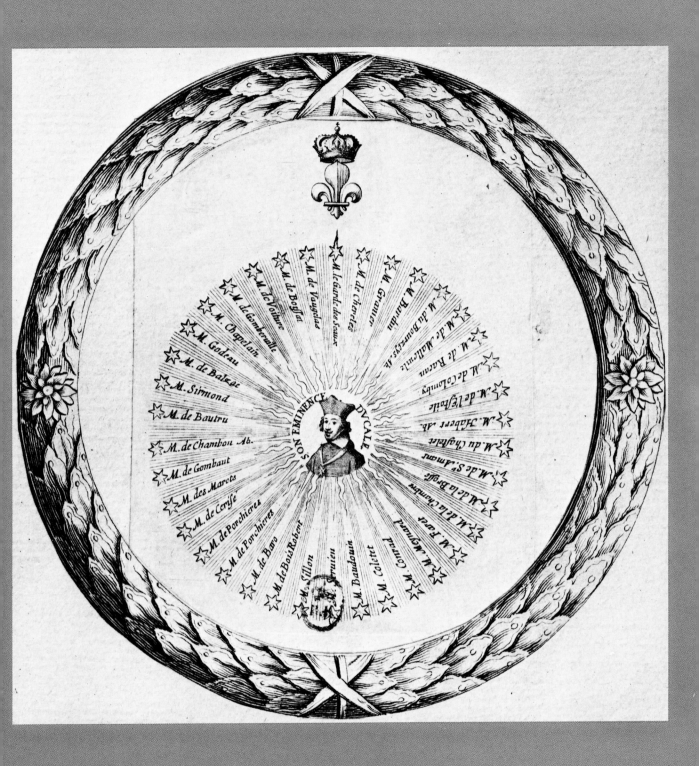

Richelieu as the sun beaming upon the stars of the aca-
demicians. (Bibliothèque Nationale, Paris. *Photo Giraudon*)

The siege of Arras. (Bibliothèque Nationale, Paris. *Photo Documentation Française*)

E DES ESPAIGNOLS A L'ATTAQVE DES LIGNES DV
RIVEE DV CONVOY, ET LA REDDITION DE LA VILLE
RAS A L'OBEISSANCE DV ROY.

ARRAS

Entrée des François

le Duc de Chaulne

le Duc d'Anguien

de la Mestleraye   Mr. du Hallier   l'arrivée   du Controy

Mr. le grand Escuyer

le Mr. de Chastillou

B.R Boudan excudit Cum Priuil Regis   les Ducs de Beaufort de Mercœur de Nemours et de Luynes.

XIV

The War with Spain

Grotius, the Dutch authority on international law, was in the service of the Swedish government. Richelieu, who did not much relish bargaining with a mind as good as his own, found him tough and tricky to deal with and dreaded his visits. But they did come to terms on the subject of the war in Germany. It is depressing to consider the long, secret talks between the philosopher of the law of nations and a Catholic cardinal dedicated to the continuation of lawlessness and disorder throughout the empire while French troops were engaged with Spain. But for both of them, there was one moral standard for princes and quite another for private persons. This was the crux of Richelieu's philosophy. He recognized the dangers of the double standard, but these dangers simply dictated that there was no room in politics for little men. Only a great man could be trusted to reconcile a life of personal rectitude with one where murder for the state was on occasion required, particularly murder of little men, like Louis de Marillac, who aspired to offices for which they were not qualified.

For the first couple of years everything went wrong in the great war that Richelieu had started in 1635. France's northern frontier was invaded by the Spaniards and her eastern by the constant pest, Duke Charles of Lorraine. Furthermore, the Swedish government delayed ratification of Richelieu's arrangements with their envoy, and for this period the Swedes did little in Germany. In 1636 the Spaniards crossed the Somme and occupied the town of Corbie, only eighty miles from Paris. Refugees poured into the capital, and Richelieu saw his long

NATUS
1583

OBIIT
1645

HUGO GROTIUS

Hugo Grotius. (Musée Condé, Chantilly. *Photo Giraudon*)

nightmare about to be executed. Paris would be occupied by the Habsburgs! Was *this* the fruit of his years of toil?

For once he lost his head. He advocated moving the government south. Louis XIII showed himself king indeed and refused. Père Joseph, behind the closed doors of the Palais-Cardinal, worked on his friend until he was pulled together. Richelieu drove, unguarded, through the streets of Paris. There were even cheers. Then he followed Louis XIII north. They were both before Corbie when the French forces retook the town.

By the end of 1637 the Spanish invasion of northern France had been repulsed, and in the south the duc d'Enghien had cleared the Spaniards from French soil. Sweden became active again in the war, and in the Low Lands the Dutch retook Breda. Bernard of Saxe-Weimar, the French-subsidized leader of the anti-Imperial forces in Germany, captured Breisach in 1638. Shortly afterward this rather too successful *condottiere* died and removed himself as an inconvenient candidate for the Alsatian throne. Like Gustavus Adolphus he had the courtesy not to survive his utility to France.

The war could now be carried into northern Spain at both ends of the Pyrenees. By the happiest of coincidences Catalonia took this moment to mount a full-scale rebellion against Philip IV. The Catalonians even wanted to recognize Louis XIII as their sovereign. This was going a bit far for Richelieu, who was a great believer in not overextending his frontiers, but he subsidized the rebels. In the end the uprising was bloodily suppressed, but not before it had accomplished Richelieu's purposes. Spanish forces had to be diverted from all fronts to be used in the civil war. Then Portugal revolted, and Richelieu, of course, seized on this, too. Spain, at long last, began to collapse, bringing Olivares down in the general ruin. The legend of Spanish invincibility on land was extinguished as completely as it had been at sea with the defeat of its Armada. In little more than half a century, Louis XIV would be able to put his grandson on the throne of Philip II.

Toward the end of Richelieu's life all the pieces of his puzzle began to fall into place. The war would go on long after his death, but the decisive victories came before. In the north, Arras surrendered, and

L'ASYLE DES OPPRESSEZ.

Le Roy de Portugal.

Grand Roy toujours vainqueur, nous peuples oppressez,
Implorons le secours de vos puissantes armes,
Nostre Prince aujourd'huy se mocque de nos larmes,
Et tous les Catalans y sont interessez.

Monarque Belliqueux, le Roy de Portugal
Se presente à vos yeux, donnez de l'allegrance
A son peuple foulé, tirez le de souffrance,
Vous le pouvez Grand Roy, avons nul est esgal.

Above: Louis XIII with open arms offering asylum to the oppressed Catalonia. *Below:* Louis XIII's victorious homecoming after the reddition of Collioure and Perpignan. (Bibliothèque Nationale, Paris)

HEVREVX RETOVR DV ROY LOVIS TRES CHRESTIEN APRES AVOIRE REDVIT A SON OBEISSANCE LES VILLES DE COLLIORRE ET PERPIGNAN

enfin de ma valeur iay fait voir la puissance,
l'orgueil des Espagnols à mes loix est soumis
et perpignan reduit a mon obeissance
A reppandu l'effroy ches tous mes ennemis,

Magnanime Heros ta derniere victoire
Où de mes ennemis renil les Estas mourans
Me couronne le front des raisons de ta gloire,
et destruit les proiets des orgueilleux Tirans

Princes que le destin à la France prepare,
Au Roy Victorieux a donne pour enfans
Courés d'un pas leger embrasser vostre pere,
Et voyes sur son front des lauriers Triomphans

1641

La France

Right: "Surrender of Breda" in 1625 to the Spanish, by Velázquez. It was retaken by the Dutch in 1638. (The Prado Museum, Madrid.) *Below:* Town of Breisach. (*Photo Documentation Française*).

G. A. Böckler delineau.

the province of Artois was united to France. In 1641 Charles of Lorraine fled to Flanders to join the Spanish army, and France reoccupied all his territories. The duc de Bouillon was caught in another conspiracy, and France took over permanently his principality of Sedan. In Italy, it is true, French interests did not prosper—Richelieu was forced to evacuate Savoy, and the famous Valtelline was reoccupied by Spain— but what did he care about Italy when the Habsburg power was broken?

Thus Richelieu was justified in telling the king, when the latter visited him on his deathbed at the end of 1642, that the enemies of France were everywhere in retreat. Neither man lived to see the final results of the war in the Treaties of Westphalia (1648) and of the Pyrenees (1659) when the present borders of France were approximately established, but these results were already anticipated. What Richelieu did not see fit to add to his summation to the king was that the treasury was depleted by the huge costs of war and foreign subsidies, and that the condition of the lower classes was pitiable. Did such things count? Those in the business of achieving *gloire* had to be prepared to pay the toll. Richelieu certainly was. He had only impatience with the carping critics who weighed present misery against future magnificence.

198

Don Gaspar de Guzmán, Conde-Duque de Olivares, by Velázquez. (Art Museum, São Paulo. *Photo Giraudon*)

VEVE GENERALE EN PERSPECTIVE DV CHASTEAV, DES BASSE

Opposite and above: The Orangerie and the Cascades in the Park of Richelieu's Château in Rueil. *Below:* Château de Richelieu. (Musée Carnavalet, Paris. *Photos Larousse*)

L'ANTI-COVR, DES PARTERRES, DES IARDINS, &C. DE RICHELIEV.

XV

Richelieu's Wealth and Houses

I t is ironical to recall that Richelieu's first public speech, addressed to the throne at the meeting of the Estates-General in 1615, contained the suggestion to the queen-mother that priests should be called to the cabinet because, with minds undistracted from the hereafter by family ties, they would not be concerned with material gain. Yet the undistracted priest Richelieu, who entered public life a relatively poor man, was to die one of the richest in Europe.

It has been said by his worshipers that he believed that only by living in state could a governor hold the respect of the governed, that the glory of his palaces and retinues was simply the reflected glory of the nation that he represented. There may have been some truth in this, particularly in the baroque age in which he lived, but surely the public would have been sufficiently impressed by one palace in Paris and a troop of horse guards. Did he have to have another at Rueil? And did he have to build a third, the biggest in France, in a spot so secluded from the very public that he was supposed to be impressing that it was necessary to erect a whole new town at its gates?

No, it is simpler to admit at once that Richelieu was avaricious, with the peculiar avariciousness of the nobleman who has spent his youth seeing his family trying to look properly grand on a woefully inadequate income. There never seems to be enough luxury in the world to satisfy this particular brand of early frustration. Besides, Richelieu lived in an era that might have been known as the age of favorites. Never before or since have states been so plundered. Consider what the

Heroic statue of Louis XIII in the Place des Vosges. This is a reproduction of the 1639 statue shown on page 70.
(Photo Richard Kalvar/VIVA)

duke of Buckingham got out of two kings of England. Consider the titanic fortune that Lerma obtained from Philip III of Spain, and of the even greater one that Olivares got from Philip IV. Think of the Barberini in Rome, those "undistracted" priests, whose extravagance scandalized a city that had regarded itself as incapable of further scandalization by papal nephews. And, finally, look at Wallenstein in Germany whose private army made the emperor at last tremble for his very throne. It was the order of the day for politicians to enrich themselves, and Richelieu certainly followed that order. The difference between him and the others was, as with his morals, in his sublime confidence that the glory of France was identical with the glory of Richelieu. It gave a weird consistency and an odd splendor to everything he did. Even when he bought a picture, he was doing it for France.

How did he make his fortune? Mostly by royal grants. Louis XIII, however personally parsimonious, probably did not much care how many benefices his first minister took. He made Richelieu twice a duke, of Richelieu and of Fronsac; he gave him the barony of La Ferté-Bernard; the governments of Honfleur and Le Havre; the port rights of La Rochelle; the salt revenues of Brouage; the abbeys of Cluny, Saint-Riquier, and some eight others; the revenues of the galleys; the revenues of the admiralty—there seemed no end to it. Richelieu's income has been estimated as high as three million livres. It is true that some of this he placed at the disposal of the State in times of emergency, when cash was scarce, but this was only common sense, for his continued wealth depended entirely on the success of his national policy. One is sure that he always paid himself back.

His residence in Paris was the Palais-Cardinal, now the Palais-Royal, on the Rue Saint-Honoré. It was designed by Lemercier in 1620 and completed in 1633. Very little of the original edifice remains, but it was sumptuous enough to arouse the jealousy of the king to whom Richelieu prudently transferred the legal title. The hall was decorated with allegorical canvases by Champaigne and Vouet showing France heaping up her riches at the feet of the cardinal as he sits enthroned with Justice, Piety, and Wisdom. The Gallery of Great Men contained twenty-six portraits, greater than life size, of historic figures from

Suger, medieval abbot of Saint-Denis, to Louis XIII. In the library there was another gallery of Roman portrait busts and a huge collection, one of three finest in Europe, of books and manuscripts, all bound in red morocco and stamped with the arms of the cardinal. The chapel contained his unique assemblage of jewels and religious plate, and the Grand Cabinet with its paintings by Andrea del Sarto and Poussin, and its Leonardo's *Saint Anne* was the admiration of Paris. One inventory of the Palais-Cardinal lists five hundred pictures, including those by Raphael, Titian, Leonardo, Solario, Giulio Romano, Luini, Giovanni Bellini, Corregio, Albano, Poussin, Claude, Rubens, and Champaigne. There were antique statues and bronzes, tapestries, Persian rugs, Florentine tables of mosaic and porphyry, and even Chinese lacquers and ceramics.

To escape the city and still be near the king when he went to Saint-Germain, Richelieu purchased and embellished the château de Rueil. Here he concentrated on the grounds. His concern for trees amounted almost to a passion. He was constantly writing those in charge of his landscaping not to cut down any more than was absolutely essential. When he was too ill to go outside, he would sit by an open window where he could look out at the gardens, and his features would relax at the vision of greenswards, of multicolored roses in ordered squares, of violet-white tulips, of thick foliage on the Grande Allée, and of the tall Indian chestnuts which cast their shadows over the pond, which he had imported and which came to be known as "cardinals."

But his great memorial, his pyramid, was to have been the château de Richelieu, of which only one pavilion survives. It was completed but not in time for him to occupy it, and it must have been one of the wonders of the seventeenth-century world. It was erected on the site of a small château in which he had lived as a child, near Chinon in Poitou. This château was presumably leveled, although there is some evidence that the chamber where Richelieu was born (if he was not born, as some historians claim, in Paris) was preserved. Indeed, the Grande Mademoiselle (Gaston's daughter and no friend to Richelieu) speaks of this piece of vanity as wrecking the dimensions of the central pavilion.

Opposite: "Slave" by Michelangelo. This and all the other paintings and sculpture in this chapter were originally in the Cardinal's collection. (*Photo Richard Kalvar/VIVA*). *Above:* The Palais-Cardinal, Paris. This was converted into the present Palais-Royal. (Bibliothèque Nationale, Paris. *Photo Larousse*). *Below:* The anchor, emblem of Richelieu's naval administration, can still be seen on the walls of the Palais-Royal. (*Photo Richard Kalvar/VIVA*)

Opposite: "Saint Anne and the Virgin" by Leonardo da Vinci.
(Musée du Louvre. *Photo Chuzeville*). *Above:* "Le Parnasse"
by Andrea Mantegna (Musée du Louvre. *Photo Giraudon*)

Opposite: "The Triumph of Bacchus" by Nicolas Poussin. (Nelson Gallery, Atkins Museum/Nelson Fund, Kansas City, Mo.) *Above:* "The Birth of Venus" by Nicolas Poussin. (Philadelphia Museum of Art: The George W. Elkins Collection)

As the cardinal's household consisted of some fifteen hundred souls, and as many more could be expected to congregate around the residence of so great a statesman, and as accommodations had always to be available for the king and *his* household, a town was constructed to supplement the château. Some of this survives, a charming red-brick Louis XIII creation, reminiscent of the Place des Vosges in Paris. The main avenue was composed of twenty-eight houses for the principal officers of the cardinal's household. The town was designed symmetrically, like Versailles, into a series of courts and forecourts for the stables and service buildings, all moving toward the climax of the magnificent main gate of the château, which was decorated with statues and pyramids and surmounted by a heroic marble statue of Louis XIII. Over the principal entrance of the central pavilion, seen through the gate, in niches, were the two marble slaves of Michelangelo, now in the Louvre, and originally designed for the tomb of Julius II, which had been bequeathed to the cardinal by the unfortunate duc de Montmorency. Around the Court of Honor were sixty antique Roman statues that Richelieu had been allowed to take from the Holy See by Urban VIII, the same pontiff who had used the Pantheon as a quarry for the embellishment of Saint Peter's.

Inside the main pavilion a great stairway of porphyry rose in a double spiral to the state apartments where, among other treasures, a visitor might see: *The Flight into Egypt*, a Dürer triptych, *Parnassus* by Mantegna, *Combat of Love and Chastity* by Perugino, *The Triumph of Neptune* by Poussin (now in the Philadelphia Museum and perhaps the artist's greatest picture), *Saint Sebastian* and *Saint Francis* by Caracci. The Grande Galerie had twenty murals, ten on each side, representing the *Conquests of Louis XIII under the Ministry of Richelieu*. One wonders what the king would have thought of these had his contemplated visits ever taken place.

The wanderer today in the great green enclosure where the château de Richelieu once stood, coming upon the lonely surviving pavilion, may recall the final lines of "Ozymandias," Shelley's famous sonnet on the futility of pomp. But one doubts if the château, even had it survived until today, would have been Richelieu's monument. It was

Doors from Château de Richelieu. Note again the emblem of the anchor. (*Photo Richard Kalvar/VIVA*)

Recent photographs of the Town of Richelieu. (*Photos Richard Kalvar/VIVA*)

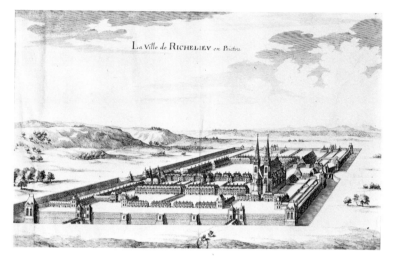

La Ville de RICHELIEV en Poictou.

Further views of the Town of Richelieu. The engraving on the opposite page was done in the 17th century. Photograph at left shows the only remaining pavilion of the Château de Richelieu. (*Photos Richard Kalvar/VIVA*)

never an edifice of great beauty; it had been too occupied with the business of impressing its beholders. Richelieu's true monument is—to the extent, anyway, that he made his contribution to it—French culture, in all its order and grace. If it was founded on political repression and military conquest, it has still gloriously survived those things. The fact that too heavy a price may have been paid for it is no reason not to venerate the result.

Preceding page: Architectural detail, Town of Richelieu. *Right:* The Park, Château de Richelieu. (*Photos Richard Kalvar/VIVA*)

XVI

Richelieu's Family

Richelieu had the usual problem of the self-made man: the family that he raised to greatness did not possess his own extraordinary qualities. Yet he did the best that he could with his material. He had in a virulent form the disease that commonly infests the lesser nobility: he wanted the Richelieus to join the ranks of the greatest French families: the Rohans, the Montmorencys, the La Trémoilles. To some extent he succeeded.

Unlike those of the Renaissance popes, his nephews and nieces were what they purported to be and not disguised bastards. The cardinal had two brothers and two sisters, but only the latter had issue, so the name and titles of Richelieu had to be passed down the distaff side. The cardinal's eldest brother, the marquis de Richelieu, had, as we have seen, died in a duel. He was probably the ablest of the family, after Armand, and had been indispensable at court in the early days promoting his younger brother's fortune. He had accompanied the fallen minister to Avignon and helped to engineer his return to power. Armand seems to have loved and trusted as well as admired him. Had the marquis survived, he would certainly have been one of the great men of the realm.

It was different with Richelieu's second older brother. Alphonse's decision to become a monk had originally necessitated Armand's transfer from a military to a clerical life. He was a man of intense

224

ALPHONSVS CARDINALIS
ARCHIEPVS. LVGDVN.

C. Mellan Gall' del. et ʃ.   Romæ ʃup. pm.
1.6.3.6.

Alphonse du Plessis, Cardinal and archbishop of Lyon. (Bibliothèque Nationale, Paris. *Photo Giraudon*)

religious feeling, perhaps something of a mystic, but his feeling took him on occasion to the borderline of sanity. He had delusions of omnipotence. He must, however, have had some executive capacity, for Armand would not suffer him to remain in seclusion but removed him from his monastery to make him a cardinal and archbishop of Lyon. He also used him in the vital post of ambassador to the Vatican. Alphonse's appointments may be further evidence of the enormous role that personal trustworthiness played in Richelieu's promotions. In a day when it was not uncommon for the crown to be betrayed in foreign courts by its own diplomatic corps, an ounce of reliability was worth a pound of brains. This factor, as well as the desire for family aggrandizement, may have been behind much of the nepotism of the times. Richelieu's need for security in his domestic and political household was a constant preoccupation. There were times when it almost seemed his only requirement of a human relationship. "*I* will provide the brains and the plan," he seemed to be saying, "if *you* will only be loyal."

The cardinal's favorite relative was his niece, Marie-Madeleine de Combalet, who lived with him and helped to run his household. She was the daughter of his older sister, Françoise, and René Vignerot de Pont-Courlay and had been married to a nephew of Luynes who had died in combat. Although a widow much sought in marriage, she preferred to enter a convent and was dissuaded only by the urgent plea of her uncle, who wanted her in his own household and created her, in her own right, duchesse d'Aiguillon. Thereafter she affected a costume that seemed a compromise between the garb of a Carmelite nun and the dress of a great lady. It was said that she hid her ambition under a mask of piety and false modesty. "Subtle, artificial, out for herself" was Mazarin's description of her. She was mannered but bright, smart but precious. One is not surprised to learn that she was a pillar of the hôtel de Rambouillet. She seems to have stepped out of Molière, either from *Les Précieuses Ridicules* or *Tartuffe*.

Did Richelieu dream of marrying her to Gaston? Would he have dared? It was said at the time that Louis XIII got wind of the idea and made it clear that he would not tolerate a sister-in-law so lowborn. We shall never know. But it is certain that Gaston paid at least some equivocal attention to Madeleine for Richelieu wrote to warn him off:

> I don't know if I should rejoice and thank you for the honor that it has pleased Your Highness to bestow on my niece, being in doubt as to whether it is because you think she may become the sort of woman that you have hitherto expected women to be or because you have at last learned to respect ladies of rank.

It is only fair to Madeleine to point out that in the thirty-three years that she survived her uncle she obtained the reputation in Paris of a great lady of charity. It was to the descendants of her brother, François de Vignerot, sieur de Pont-Courlay, that the title and principal wealth of Richelieu passed.

The cardinal's younger sister, Nicole, who died insane, had been married to Urbain de Maillé, marquis de Brézé, whose fortunes her brother took pains to promote despite his arrogant and difficult personality. He became a marshal of France and governor of Anjou and Brittany. His son, Armand, inherited the cardinal's second duchy, Fronsac, and became an admiral at an early age, but his brilliant career was cut short by his death at the siege of Orbitello in 1646, and his title and wealth went back to the Richelieus of the Vignerot or Pont-Courlay branch.

It was through the second child of the Brézés, Claire Clémence, that the cardinal achieved his greatest dynastic ambition. Her life is the tragic story of a pawn. As a child she was totally neglected by a lunatic mother and a heartless father and brought up by servants under the distant guidance of the cardinal. When she was still a child, playing with dolls, she was engaged to the duc d'Enghien, son and heir of the prince de Condé, a young man who already had a military reputation and who was later to be the mighty general known as the *Grand* Condé. As a match it was almost incredibly splendid. The Condés were Bourbons of a cadet branch; only the lives of the king, his two infant sons, and Gaston stood between them and the crown. Claire had a reasonable chance of becoming queen of France, but no chance at all of being happy.

Her husband despised her from the start. He had been forced

to wed her by his avaricious father, who was in hot pursuit of the cardinal's fortune (which, incidentally, the Condés never got), and he was deeply and permanently humiliated by such a misalliance. It was all very well for the cardinal to maintain that in royal houses only the male line counted (Marie de Médicis was always regarded as a banker's daughter, even though on her mother's side she was a granddaughter of Emperor Ferdinand I), but Louis de Bourbon, duc d'Enghien, had stricter views. Besides, his bride was immature and dwarfish. The great ladies giggled at her awkwardness, even at the Palais-Cardinal. Poor little Claire had united the Richelieus and the Bourbons and would live in hell for her pains.

The rest of her story is sad to relate. She was in love with her frosty hero of a husband and did everything in her power to win his affection. She cared nothing for the cardinal's principles and became a passionate *frondeuse* after his death. When her husband was jailed in Vincennes by Mazarin, she raised his standard in Bordeaux and rallied his followers. It was like a bad historical movie, except that the hero was not won over in the end. When peace was restored, Condé lived largely apart from her. Finally he took advantage of the scandal aroused by an unseemly fight at Chantilly between an usher of her household and a gentleman of the Condé entourage to deprive her of her son and lock her up permanently in the château de Châteauroux. The excuse was that the fight had been over her favors. As all the evidence was suppressed we can never know what happened. Claire lived on in captivity until 1694. When she died, she was completely insane.

There is some satisfaction in considering that Condé, who died in 1686, lived long enough to witness the forced marriage of his grandson and heir to a bastard of Louis XIV. Had he survived another six years, he would have had the dubious pleasure of seeing his granddaughter married to another royal bastard. The Condé blood was forever polluted in the minds of the purer royalists. At least Claire had been legitimate.

Richelieu's will contained a carefully designed estate plan to perpetuate the glory of his family. Claire had had her dowry; she was left nothing. The Condés litigated the matter at great length but un-

Opposite above: Urbain de Maillé, marquis de Brézé. (*Photo Larousse*). *Opposite below:* Louis de Bourbon, duc d'Enghien, later prince de Condé (Le Grand Condé). (*Photo Richard Kalvar/VIVA*)

successfully. The duchesse d'Aiguillon was left a large cash bequest. But her brother François was bypassed in favor of his eldest son, Armand, who received the duchy of Richelieu and its revenues provided that he should assume the title and pay his father an annuity of thirty thousand livres. To Claire's brother Armand de Maillé went the duchy of Fronsac. It was provided that each duchy would go to the holder of the other in default of heirs male, and on Armand de Maillé's death the two duchies were reunited in the Vignerot line. Once again the Condés unsuccessfully litigated. Richelieu's final testamentary warning to his family affirmed his faith in the nobility whose force he had curbed but whose function he still considered essential to France.

> I forbid my heirs to marry into houses that are not truly noble, having rendered them independent that they might have more regard for birth and virtue than for goods and riches.

That has always been the pale little faith of the accumulator. In Richelieu's case, as in others, it was largely unjustified by his posterity. He did better, however, than some. Almost two hundred years after his death a duc de Richelieu was again first minister of France.

Le Grand Condé, by Juste d'Egmont. (Musée Condé, Chantilly. *Photo Giraudon*)

XVII

The King's Confessor

The peace party were not all pro-Spanish. There were voices in the church that cried for an armistice because Catholics were fighting Catholics. Saint Vincent-de-Paul threw himself on his knees before Richelieu and cried in a tear-choked voice: "Peace, my lord, give us peace! Have pity on us—give peace to France!" The cardinal appeared moved by his description of the miseries of the people and raised him to his feet saying: "I too, Monsieur Vincent, am working for the peace of Europe, but, alas, it does not depend on me alone." He could cope with Monsieur Vincent handily enough, for the latter was not privy to the king. But when a cleric close to Louis XIII got the idea into his head that God had appointed him the peacemaker of Europe, Richelieu had to act quickly. And when that cleric happened to be the king's confessor, he could hardly act quickly enough.

He had the initial advantage of being able to appoint this officer, and he inclined to appoint him from the Jesuits, provided the candidate understood just what was expected of him. He was expected to give the king absolution without interfering in any way in affairs of state. In 1637 Richelieu selected a sincere but simple soul, one père Caussin. He thought he had his man. As events turned out, he could not have been more wrong.

For père Caussin held as an article of faith that a sovereign could not make a complete confession without hashing over every detail of his royal function and responsibility. How could Richelieu have missed so vital a point when he screened the candidate? Undoubtedly because Caussin deliberately deceived him. The latter seems to have fancied himself a new Jeanne d'Arc sent to save France from

1576. St VINCENT de PAUL, fondateur et 1er Général. 1660.

Saint Vincent de Paul. (*Photo Larousse*)

the policies of a cynical minister who was using heretics and Turks in an unholy war against the true faith. Obviously, he would have to conceal such views until he had his appointment.

Louis XIII at just this time was greatly intrigued with a lady-in-waiting of the queen, Mademoiselle de La Fayette. It was, as we have seen, one of his strange platonic attractions, but its eighteen-year-old object could not be expected to understand this. She was a beautiful, serious, high-minded girl, devoted to the queen and even more devoted to her church, and she took it for granted that the king wanted to make her his mistress. To avoid becoming a royal concubine she was determined to become a nun, and Richelieu, who suspected that any incorruptible friend of Anne of Austria could only be his own enemy, was equally determined to speed her in her vocation. In his first interview with the new confessor he instructed him to suggest to the king that a girl so religiously inclined should be encouraged to abandon the world. He thereafter sent Sublet des Noyers, one of his faithful creatures, to put the matter even more forcefully. Noyers told Caussin that Mademoiselle de La Fayette was a designing hussy who would make all kinds of trouble and that nothing should be done to hinder a religious retreat so happily inspired.

Caussin was shocked, but he was careful not to show it. He examined Mademoiselle de La Fayette meticulously on her religious vocation and was bold enough to point out to her that she might be able to serve God as well in court as in a cloister. But when the girl had convinced him that her vocation was genuine, he was delighted, at least in his capacity as a priest, and he told the cardinal so. Richelieu, of course, was also delighted, but he was concerned over the possibility of the least delay. He suggested that another of his creatures, a priest bound to him by oath, père Carré, be dispatched to the would-be nun to confirm her in her resolution. Caussin countered with the argument that the use of too many agents might alert the king to the pressure placed on his young favorite. Carré was called off, and the girl was let alone.

Mademoiselle de La Fayette certainly needed no confirmation. She now requested the king's permission to be received into the Convent of the Visitation in Paris without even waiting for her parents' consent. Louis XIII granted her prayer but fell into a deep depression. Richelieu, alarmed, wrote him that sovereigns who did their duty were recompensed not only in heaven but on this earth! Mademoiselle de La Fayette appeared at the queen's levee and told all present that she was taking the name of Sister Marie as she could not, after serving so great and good a mistress, pick a lesser one. Everyone was much affected, and the king entered, tears in his eyes. The girl greeted him by saying that the greatest of his favors had been his permission to allow her to devote herself to God. It was a touching scene. Had Richelieu been present, his facile tears would have been most appropriate.

The cardinal submitted a memorandum to Louis about one Mademoiselle de Chemerault, who had been consulted by a priest and who was willing to take Mademoiselle de La Fayette's place, willing, indeed, to go a lot further. Louis spurned the unworthy suggestion. He went in to Paris and had long talks with Sister Marie through the grille at the convent. It was just the way he liked matters to be with his women. Richelieu was much agitated by these visits and admitted to Caussin that the first of them had taken place without his knowledge. This was a rare admission, for the cardinal liked everyone to believe that he was on notice of the king's smallest plan. According to Caussin's later account, Richelieu was particularly smooth and benevolent at this interview, promising the Jesuit great things and impressing on him the importance of their working together. When Caussin suggested that the cardinal might have exaggerated the importance of Mademoiselle de La Fayette, that she was only, after all, an innocent child, Richelieu retorted: "You are naïve. You don't know the malice of the world. Take it from me, that 'child' almost ruined everything."

Caussin indeed was naïve, but not as Richelieu professed to suppose. He was naïve not to see that the cardinal was already "on" to him.

The royal confessor and Mademoiselle de La Fayette now entered on an active campaign to appeal to Louis' conscience as a Christian to abandon the "abominable crime" of supporting heretics in Germany and infidels in the Mediterranean. She worked through the grille; he through the confessional. He wrote her that if he were sent to the Bastille he would continue to pray with her as an "accomplice and neighbor." The "neighbor" was a reference to the proximity of the Bastille to the Convent of the Visitation. Richelieu, who at all times had access to the royal cabinet, continually marched in when Caussin was closeted with the king. The two "conspirators" would instantly drop their talk of international affairs and pretend to be concerned with the holy texts opened on the table before them.

Caussin's description of the king's complaints about Richelieu bears the ring of truth. We know how Louis loved to denigrate his mighty minister. He told Caussin that Richelieu was a tyrant not only to his people but to him, that he spread misery and poverty throughout France while enriching himself, that he paid no attention whatever to his duties as a priest, regarding his benefices as so many assets, and that he made the poor king spend all his time at Saint-Germain because he liked his own nearby château at Rueil!

When Richelieu at last struck, he struck quickly. He summoned Caussin to Rueil, and informed him icily that he knew all about his relations with Mademoiselle de La Fayette. He warned him that a virtuous man should guard against the artifices of women. While they were talking, they heard a clatter in the courtyard. "The king is coming!" Richelieu cried. "He must not find us together. You know how suspicious he is. Go out by this little stairway!" Caussin, like the fool he was, went out. Later, when the king had departed, he was told that the cardinal would not see him again.

Apparently Louis had asked for Caussin and been told that he was not there. Then the cardinal, in an impassioned lecture, had reviewed his whole domestic and foreign policy, assailing the king with unanswerable arguments—at least ones that Louis could not answer—and ending with the ultimatum that Louis must choose between his confessor and his minister. This, of course, was Richelieu's old ace of trumps, but he never played it unless he had to. It was Caussin's brief and final glory that he had forced the cardinal's hand.

Caussin was able to see the king once more, and he wisely staked his whole case on personal devotion. "I quit Your Majesty with the deepest regret!" he exclaimed. "To my dying breath I shall dedicate my prayers to Your Majesty's salvation!" Louis was showing signs of emotion when Chavigny and Noyers, both Richelieu's men, suddenly walked in. Caussin withdrew and went to Paris. Immediately thereafter he was exiled to Rennes. All his books and papers were confiscated. Luckily for him, the king had stipulated that nothing was to happen to his person. The royal visits to Sister Marie were discontinued.

On September 5, 1638, after twenty years of a childless marriage, Queen Anne gave birth to the future Louis XIV, and the whole kingdom burst into jubilation. But nobody was more jubilant than poor exiled Caussin. He attributed the event entirely to the pious counsels of Mademoiselle de La Fayette who had never ceased to urge the king toward a "holy and cordial" love for his spouse. "O little Deborah!" he wrote, transported to biblical analogies. "You have every reason to praise your sovereign whom I honor for having followed your precepts! Praise be to God who has rendered this young woman capable, by sacrificing a king's love, of making herself the mother of nations!"

Caussin probably exaggerated Deborah's role. Louis and Anne had had sexual relations earlier in their marriage, but these had been discontinued after Anne's miscarriage. Louis had blamed the event on her folly in running about the Louvre with her ladies and had taken the peculiar revenge of deserting her bed. But on a December night in 1637, when he was passing through Paris en route from Versailles to Saint-Maur, he had paused to call on Mademoiselle de La Fayette at her convent. During the visit a great storm had broken out, and it was soon evident that the king could neither go on to Saint-Maur nor return to Versailles. His own apartments at the Louvre were not ready, and the captain of his guard suggested that he repair to the queen's. Louis retorted in surly fashion that the queen supped and retired too late for him. The storm, however, grew worse, and he was at last constrained to change his mind. The queen, delighted, gave him an excellent supper, and they went to bed together. In due course the future sun king appeared. It does not appear that Mademoiselle de La Fayette participated in the discussion of where the night should be spent.

In 1639, far from the court and after a year's reflection on the turbulent events that had placed him so close to the pulse of power, Caussin penned this devastating portrait of the cardinal:

His intelligence is remarkable, and always leaps to the outer limit of a subject—without always going through the middle. He is rather big than great, rather haughty than high, rather proud than generous. His subtlety exceeds his prudence.

Nature and art have both made him changeable. His heart is full of labyrinths which he hides from the world—and sometimes from himself.

He never shows a particular side of his character to more than one person at a time—for fear of giving them a foothold on his nature. He is bold with the timid and timid with the bold. One moment sees him happily expansive; another in a fury.

His demeanor is gracious and his tongue flattering. He is all smiles to those whom he wishes to win and terrible to those he has won.

He bounds his pledges by his own interests; they say his promises are writ on sand. What he talks of most is frequently what he least wishes. He expects you to guess what he wants, and you are punished if you guess wrong.

He hates generous, open-hearted souls and despises those who worship him. His bad temper makes him insupportable to his friends and irreconcilable to his enemies. He takes credit for all that comes out well and throws the blame for misfortune on others.

If he wanted to be only one of the great, that might pass, but as he wants to be the only great one, he exposes himself to the jealousies of all the world.

He loves literature and favors the arts but only to have more valets and flatterers.

If he defends the authority of the king, it is only to forward his own.

We must remember that it is a victim's judgment.

Richelieu holding the founding charter of the Académie Française. (*Photo Richard Kalvar/VIVA*)

Panorama of Paris showing Louis XIII and Anne of Austria. (*Photo Larousse*)

XVIII

Cinq-Mars

The conspiracy of Cinq-Mars always looms large in histories and biographies of the cardinal. Perhaps it is because it comes at the end of Richelieu's life—the last conspiracy and the final victory. Perhaps it is because of the romantic and dashing figure of Cinq-Mars, a forecast of the fiction of Dumas. Perhaps it is simply because the tale is such a dramatic one.

The king's second and final lady friend, Mademoiselle de Hautefort, was in declining favor in 1639. She had none of Mademoiselle de La Fayette's fear of becoming a royal concubine, but she had no desire to become one. Louis was not an attractive prospect as a lover. Once he had spat a mouthful of wine into the bosom of the lady next to him at table whose dress, in his opinion, had been cut too low. Mademoiselle de Hautefort, a close and loyal friend of the queen, was quite content with a political role. She was out for what all the other anti-cardinalists had been out for: dismissal of the first minister and peace with Spain. She was a bold, bright, attractive, mocking young woman, but she was no match for Richelieu. One of her closest women friends was in his pay; he knew everything that she did.

It is a measure of Richelieu's comprehension of the king's nature that he realized that Mademoiselle de Hautefort could be more easily replaced by a man than another woman. He believed he had just the candidate. Henri d'Effiat, marquis de Cinq-Mars, was the second son of Antoine d'Effiat, a marshal of France and a loyal friend of the cardinal's. He had been brought up under Richelieu's protection after his father's early death, and his frank, loyal, and affectionate nature

Satirical drawing showing Richelieu pro-
nouncing judgment on Cinq-Mars and de Thou.

seemed to assure his devotion to his patron. He was dazzlingly good-looking and highly personable. All that Richelieu had to do was to bring him forward in court.

What happened immediately could not have been predicted by Richelieu because nothing like it had ever happened before. It had been logical to anticipate a strong, moody, rather stubborn devotion on the king's part, similar to what he had felt for Saint-Simon and for Baradas, an affection more associated with the hunting field than the council chamber. Instead of this, the king fell violently and uncharacteristically in love. Mademoiselle de Hautefort was soon blown away in the storm of the royal passion, and it even began to look as if she might not be the only casualty. Cinq-Mars, with the world suddenly at his feet, had his head turned. The title "Monsieur le Grand" which he held as master of the king's horse seemed perfectly to suit him. Could there be *two* "Messieurs le Grand" at court? He already fancied himself a statesman.

Besides, he was bored. He was a very lusty and normal young man who in no way shared the king's homoerotic tastes. Although he probably did not have to put up with much more than pawing from his royal admirer, he was expected to share the latter's dull, chaste routine. Louis' love life must have been singularly unsatisfactory. The deepest part of it was jealousy. As Goulas points out, he was like the dog in the garden who would not eat the cabbages and would not let anyone else do so. He was wildly jealous whenever Cinq-Mars went in to Paris from Saint-Germain. The latter always had an affair going and could not wait for the moment when the king retired so that he could rush off to a midnight rendezvous. To make matters worse, Louis loathed all forms of extravagance, and Cinq-Mars was an exquisite. He dressed, ate, drank, and lived on a far grander scale than the poor, stingy, infatuated king had ever dreamed of doing. The combination of boredom with intimacy finally produced contempt, and Cinq-Mars began to show his impudence in a way that no royal favorite had previously dared to.

Louis was actually reduced to complaining to the cardinal and even to the secretaries of state, Chavigny and Noyers. He wrote long, shrill memoranda, pointing out that Cinq-Mars was unbearable with his bad manners, his laziness, his impertinence, his dissipation. He accused the favorite of treating him worse than one of his own guards. It even reached the point where the king and his friend were publicly shouting at each other.

Richelieu at first could hardly take the young man seriously. Cinq-Mars, after all, had been his protégé, his creature. Was not a good scolding what he needed? When Cinq-Mars sought to enter the Royal Council, when he asked for the governorship of this or that province, when he even aspired to marry Marie de Gonzague, who was later queen of Poland, the cardinal refused him abruptly and contemptuously. As we have seen, he was never able to keep in check his inclination to be ironic and insulting. But even had he been able to do so, Cinq-Mars would probably have been equally aggrieved.

For Cinq-Mars was far too proud and too ambitious to enjoy his position as the king's *mignon*. He had no wish to go down in history in the same chapter as the friends of Henri III. He was determined to carve out a greater niche for himself as a statesman, and to do this he would obviously have to unseat his former benefactor. But he soon discovered what so many before him had learned: that however willing Louis was to listen to complaints about his first minister, he was not willing to replace him. Cinq-Mars had to fall back, as his predecessors had fallen back, on the old theory that the king, once freed of the cardinal's oppressive domination, would be only too glad to forgive and reward his liberators.

He had an intimate who encouraged him in his first dabblings in treason. François-Auguste de Thou, son of a famous historian, was a very different sort from Cinq-Mars. He was somber, homely, intellectual, and misanthropic. He had traveled widely in Europe and in the Middle East, and had known many artists and writers. He had a sultry, romantic nature that was alternately attracted by the idea of total retreat from the sordid world of men and the idea of imperially dominating that world. Like Cinq-Mars, he was haughty, with feelings that were easily hurt. He had started by admiring Richelieu and père Joseph, but he had soon felt that they had not paid enough attention to him. He was ripe for conspiracy.

The royal princes were ready too, Gaston and the comte de

Soissons, the Bourbon next in line to the throne after the Condés. They were always ready. What had they to lose? So were the border dukes, like Bouillon, with feudal loyalties divided between France and the Empire. And once these perennial discontents had made contact with Cinq-Mars and de Thou, where did they turn for troops and money? To Philip IV, of course, and to his ever-watchful minister Olivares. What did it matter to Gaston that he was dealing with an enemy in wartime? He was an old hand at this. The marquis de Fontrailles, still smarting from the cardinal's crack about his personal ugliness, was dispatched to Madrid to make a secret treaty, and the mother country was sold down the river. Olivares agreed to furnish twelve thousand soldiers and five thousand horse and as much money as necessary for the conspiracy. Gaston was promised the usual pension and another for Bouillon and Cinq-Mars. Spain was to receive Sedan from France. Fontrailles returned with the treaty sewed up in his doublet, and the conspirators were ready to move.

The cardinal at this point in the war with Spain had decided that his presence was necessary on the southern front at Roussillon. He knew perfectly well that something dangerous was brewing, but he was still lacking the sure proof needed for a conviction of treason. He could not afford to strike at Monsieur le Grand without bringing him down. Not daring to leave the king alone in Paris with the favorite, he persuaded him to take the trip south. The king and cardinal traveled separately, and both entourages were alive with rumors. Cinq-Mars became more and more openly hostile to the cardinal as the voyage progressed, and his agents everywhere were preaching dissent. It is possible that he would have struck had Richelieu in Narbonne not contracted a desperate fever from which it appeared he might not survive. The king, who had now joined the siege of Perpignan, also fell seriously sick, and Cinq-Mars decided that it might be well to get him back to Paris and to make plans for a regency council presided over by Cinq-Mars. The foolish young man suddenly saw himself rid of both king and cardinal with a splendid future opening up for himself! The king turned back north and arrived at Narbonne where he found, not Richelieu who, partially recovered, had gone on to Arles, but the two secretaries of state, Chavigny and Noyers. They had been sent back by the first minister with an urgent dispatch.

Cinq-Mars was with the king. The secretaries insisted on a private audience. Their request was granted, and Cinq-Mars withdrew. Some time afterward the two secretaries emerged from the royal chamber to reveal that the king had signed an order for the arrest of Cinq-Mars and his accomplices.

We do not know what document they carried with them that convinced Louis of his favorite's treason. It must have been very convincing for he never made the smallest effort thereafter to save the young man's neck. When Richelieu had seen it, he had called for a cup of bouillon to calm his nerves and had cried: "O God, you take great care of this kingdom and of your poor servant!" It is often assumed that the document was the secret treaty between the conspirators and Spain. But this is by no means sure as Richelieu afterward went to great lengths to obtain a copy of it from Gaston to accelerate the trials of the guilty. It is possible that it was a letter from the exiled queen-mother incriminating Cinq-Mars. How Louis would have resented any involvement between those two! At any rate, all was over.

Cinq-Mars was placed in the citadel at Montpellier. Louis XIII followed Richelieu north, taking de Thou with him. The duc de Bouillon was arrested at Casale, but like the other great ones he was let off, when he had ceded Sedan, not to Spain as he had bargained, but to his betrayed master. Gaston screamed and protested and then, as usual, confessed everything and implicated everybody.

At Tarascon the litter bearing the sick king was placed beside that of his ailing minister, and the two had a long private talk. Louis had been well prepared by Chavigny and Noyers, who had filled his ears with horror stories about the conspiracy and what the nation and the monarch himself might have escaped. One can imagine that, looking at the wise, worn, implacable face of his mistreated but always triumphant servant, Louis may have considered that some kind of final capitulation was in order. Richelieu would not have been so crude as to have said: "I told you so." No doubt he simply congratulated his master at having escaped so heinous a plot. At any rate, Louis granted all he asked. Cinq-Mars and de Thou were to be handed over to a special commission headed by Richelieu's man, chancellor Séguier. Then there could be no slip-up. The king allowed his malice full rein in the letter that he subsequently wrote to Séguier about his erstwhile loved one:

> Although this impostor and slanderer lost no occasion to set me against my cousin the cardinal, I suffered him so long as he kept himself under some degree of control. But when he went so far as to propose getting rid of my cousin and to make himself responsible for the deed, I conceived such a horror of him and such a detestation of his ideas that he had to give me up and place himself at the disposal of the king of Spain.

The trial was to be in Lyon. The king proceeded on to Paris, leaving the details to his minister. Richelieu lingered to be sure of his heads. His slow lugubrious journey up the Rhône, by barge and by litter, with the prisoner de Thou (Cinq-Mars went under separate guard) caught the imagination of many observers. Here is one account:

> He was towed up the Rhône in a barge on which had been erected a wooden cabin hung with branched crimson velvet on a background of gold. Inside this vessel was an ante-room hung in the same fashion; before and behind were ranged a number of his guards in scarlet cloaks. His Eminence lay in a bed hung with purple taffeta. Before him went a little boat to mark the fairway, and immediately behind it a boatload of arquebusiers and their officers. At every island they came to, the soldiers landed to see if there was any suspect on it and, finding none, they would mount guard on its banks until the cardinal's barge had passed by. Behind the cardinal's barge a little covered boat was attached in which was Monsieur de Thou, the king's prisoner. On the banks of the Rhône marched two companies of light cavalry. There was a fine foot regiment too which came into the cities where His Eminence was to spend the night. When his barge touched the shore, first they set up a wooden bridge from the bank to the barge. After they had tested it to see if it was safe, they took up the bed on which His Eminence lay. Six strong men carried it on two poles to the house where he was to lodge. But the strangest thing of all was that he entered the houses by the windows, for, before he came, his masons knocked down the window frames and made openings

in the walls of the rooms where he was to lodge, and built up a wooden ramp from the street to the opening in the wall of his room. In this way, in his traveling bed, he was carried through the streets and up the ramp to the room which had been prepared for him, hung by his servants with crimson and purple damask and rich furnishings. His room was guarded on all sides, there were guards in the cellars and at the doors and even in the attics.

Cinq-Mars made a full confession after being taken in by the oldest prosecutor's trick in history: he was told, quite falsely, that de Thou had talked. There was grave doubt among some of the judicial commission that de Thou was guilty of a capital crime. Some evidence pointed to the fact that he had advised the other conspirators not to enter into the treasonable treaty with Spain. But Richelieu was convinced that he was the heart and soul of the conspiracy, and he brought considerable pressure on the commission to obtain the conviction. The friends were beheaded together. Cinq-Mars made a jaunty tour of the scaffold, bowing to the crowd and waving his plumed hat; he was quite fearless. It was said that he died as a cavalier but de Thou as a Christian.

When the duc de La Rochefoucauld wrote to the cardinal, on behalf of Marie de Gonzague, to ask if she might have back her letters to Cinq-Mars and a braid of hair which she had indiscreetly given him, he opened himself up to Richelieu's most withering sarcasm. The cardinal wrote back to suggest that, because of the amplitude of the dead man's collection of braids and ladies' letters, it might be helpful if the duke's client supplied samples of both these items.

Gaston was finally broken. He had seen his mother exiled, his second marriage temporarily invalidated, and the wicked priest everywhere dominant. Furthermore, he undoubtedly considered Richelieu guilty of the murder of his two best friends. Ornano, who had been jailed in the Chalais conspiracy, had died mysteriously in prison. The same thing happened to Puylaurens who was supposed to have failed in his secret undertaking to induce Gaston to approve the rupture of his second marriage. Gaston must have felt that the cardinal was his personal devil. But he was an easygoing, happy-go-lucky fellow. His daughter, the Grande Mademoiselle, did more than anyone else to destroy his reputation as a serious man by the description of him in her memoirs as he appeared a few months after the execution of his friends in the final conspiracy:

> He had supper in my house where we had twenty-four violins.
> It was just as if Cinq-Mars and de Thou had never been.

Execution of Cinq-Mars and de Thou.

François-Auguste de Thou.

Henri d'Effiat, marquis de Cinq-Mars.

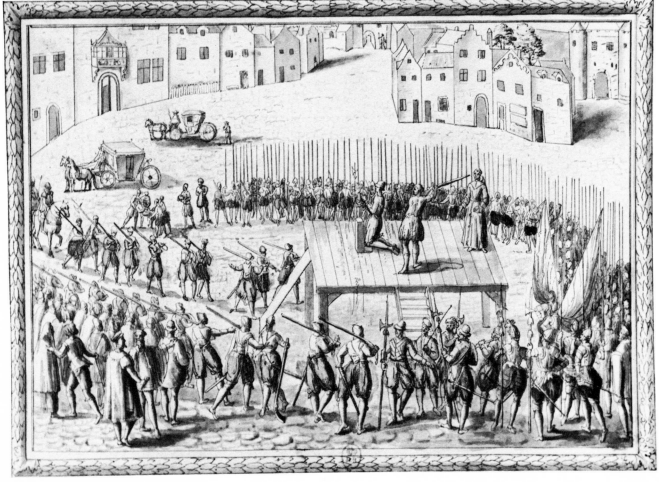

The Tuileries, the Louvre, and the Seine with a
plan for the Chartreuse de Paris borne by two
angels. (Musée du Louvre, Paris. *Photo Larousse*)

Finale

Richelieu reached Paris in November of 1642 in time to die. It seems likely that it was pneumonia that put an end at last to his many ailments. He was a prematurely old man at fifty-seven. In his bedroom at the Palais-Cardinal he faced death with perfect resignation and arranged his own affairs and those of the state in as good an order as he was able. The king came to visit him and fed him yolk of egg with his own hands, an unprecedented favor. Richelieu put off all courtly modesty on the threshold of the hereafter. He told Louis that he was leaving him his kingdom at a pinnacle of international power with all his enemies, domestic and foreign, in full retreat. He advised him to appoint Giulio Mazarin, now also a cardinal, as his successor. The king agreed.

One wonders if he would have done this had he known that Louis would survive him by only six months. Did he not remember what had happened to another pro-Spanish queen-mother with an unpopular Italian favorite? Perhaps he depended on Louis' health, ·which had always before rallied at the critical point. Perhaps, if he did not, he depended on the brilliance of Mazarin to avoid the errors of the idiotic Concini. And indeed he would have been right, for Mazarin and Anne of Austria weathered the wars of the Fronde and handed over to Louis XIV a royal authority as absolute as that which Richelieu had left them.

Asking how long he had to live and being told that twenty-four hours would settle the question one way or the other, he said with approval: "That's how to talk." He then confessed and received absolution. When asked if he had forgiven his enemies, he replied

Tomb of Richelieu in the Chapelle de la Sorbonne. The body was torn out during the Revolution, but parts of it were preserved and later restored. The skull was reinterred as late as 1972. (*Photo Richard Kalvar/VIVA*)

that he had none but those of the state. No doubt he was perfectly sincere. We have seen over and over that he had an absolute faith in the rightness of what he was doing. His fits of temper, his attacks of nerves, were all because he feared that his plans might be frustrated. Now his job was done. The Huguenots were obedient; the nobles were temporarily in order; the kingdom of Philip IV was falling apart. He could die in peace.

The room was filled with priests and courtiers. He told the duchesse d'Aiguillon to leave; he did not want her to see him die. Noting the tears in the eyes of those nearest him, he murmured: "Did you think I was immortal?" Louis XIV was to ask the same question seventy-three years later. On December 4 he slipped into a coma and died.

There was general relief, a feeling that school was out. Poor old Bassompierre was let out of the Bastille. The duc d'Enghien (the *Grand* Condé), who had blushed to be the cardinal's nephew-in-law, won the greatest victory of the war at Rocroi. In Rome the worldly old Barberini pope, Urban VIII, was reputed to have said: "If there's a God, the cardinal de Richelieu will have much to answer for. If not . . . well, he had a successful life." It was typical of the age that this same free-thinking, aristocratic prelate should have prosecuted Galileo for saying that the earth went around the sun.

2631   2526.

In the last days. (National Museum, Stockholm. *Photo Giraudon*)

Above: Deathbed portrait by Philippe de Champaigne. (Académie Française, Paris. *Photo Larousse.*) *Opposite:* The Chantilly portrait by Philippe de Champaigne. (Musée Condé, Chantilly. *Photo Giraudon*)

Le pourtrait de Monſeignr le Cardinal de Richelieu ſur ſon lit de parade, auec ſon Epitaphe.

EPITAPHE.

PASSANT, je n'oſerois preſque te dire, qui repoſe dans ce Tombeau : & j'ay peine à croire moy-meſme, que celuy puſt eſtre morel qui a fait tant d'actions immortelles. C'eſt toutefois, **LE GRAND ARMAND IEAN DV PLESSIS, CARDINAL DVC DE RICHELIEV** : Grand en Naiſſance, Grand en Pieté, Grand en Eſprit, Grand en Sageſſe, Grand en Courage, Grand en Fortune, & plus Grand encore en Vertu. Il fut bon Sujet & bon Maiſtre ; & ſçeut eſgallement obeïr & commander. Il porta la gloire de ſon Prince, par tout où il porta ſes Armes : & il porta ſes Armes, quaſi par toute l'Europe. Il n'eſt point de Rois qu'il n'ait fait trembler, ny point de Throſne où il n'euſt fait monter ſon Roy, ſi la Iuſtice n'eut conduit tous ſes deſſeins. Son illuſtre Nom ſeulement, mettoit la frayeur dans l'ame, de tous les Ennemis de l'Eſtat, & la mettra encore, dans celle de leurs Deſcendans. Si l'on contoit ſes iours par ſes Victoires, & ſes années par ſes Triomphes ; la Poſterité croiroit, qu'il auroit veſcu pluſieurs Siecles, tant il a fait des Grandes choſes : & ſon Hiſtoire n'a rien à craindre qu'elle meſme ; qui eſtant toute pleine de Prodiges & de Miracles, que l'on ne croit pas aiſément ; aura peine à perſuader aux ſiecles eſloignez du noſtre, ce qu'il a veu auec admiration. Comme il fut touſiours equitable il fut touſiours inuincible : & ſes ennemis n'ont jamais eu d'autre auantage, que le ſeul d'eſtre ſurmontés par luy. Comme il fut infiniment prudent, il fut infiniment heureux : ou pour mieux dire, il fut infiniment heureux, parce qu'il fut infiniment prudent. Comme il fut iudicieux au choix de ceux qu'il aimoit, il les rencontra ardens & fidelles : & comme il ne manquoit iamais à ſa parolle, on ne luy en a jamais guere manqué. La grandeur des euenemens, a iuſtifié la droicture de ſes intentions : & tout l'Vniuers l'a veu, l'hay de peu, aimé de pluſieurs, eſtimé de tous. Si ſes éminentes Vertus, ont fait quelquefois parler l'Enuie, la Verité l'a touſiours fait taire : & la Médiſance n'a jamais eſté crue, non pas ſeulement d'elle meſme. Il fut le Protecteur de la Vertu, & celuy de tous les beaux Arts : & par vn Miracle inoüy il fit regner les innocens plaiſirs de la Paix, au milieu des penibles trauaux de la guerre. En fin ſa reputation a eſté ſans tache : & l'on peut iuſtement l'appeler, **LE SEVL HEROS DES DERNIERS SIECLES.** Que te diray ie encore ? ſa mort a eſté digne de ſa vie. Comme il poſſedoit les richeſſes, ſans en eſtre poſſedé ; il s'en eſt detaché ſans peine : & a veu le bout de ſa carriere auec ioye, parce qu'il y voyoit des Couronnes. Il eſt mort comme il a véſcu, **GRAND INVINCIBLE, GLORIEVX**; & pour dernier honneur, **PLEVRE' DE SON ROY, PASSANT,** s'il eſt poſſible que tu ſois d'vne Climat aſſez eſloigné, pour ignorer ces éclatantes veritez, ne laiſſe pas de croire. Souuiens-toy, pour n'en pas douter, que l'on ne flatte point les Morts ; & que ie n'eſpere preſques plus rien des viuans. Si toute la France ne veut que ce Marbre luy reproche eternellement ſon ingratitude, elle te confirmera tout ce que i'ay dit **DV GRAND CARDINAL.** Va, prie, & admire toutefois en priant, Celuy que tous les Siecles admireront. Cette Inſcription a eſté Conſacrée, à l'Eternelle Memoire de ce Grand Miniſtre, par la moindre de ſes Creatures. *DE SCVDERY.*

ET comme n'ayant deſiré aucune pompe funebre, il fut porté de ſon Palais Cardinal dans vn cercueil de plomb, couuert d'vn poile de velours noir & d'vne grãd Croix de ſatin blanc & ſes armes en broderie, tenu aux 4 coins par ſes pages d'honneur, conduit par ſes Cochers & cheuaux couuerts de deuil, & Croix blanches deſſus, & ſuiuis de Meſſieurs les mareſchaux de Brezé, & la Meillerage, ſes proches parens & d'vn grand cortege de Caroſſes, plains d'vn nombre de grands Seigneurs, & de tous ſes Officiers & Domeſtiques tenans chacun des Cierges & flambeaux de cire blanche en ſi grande quantité, qu'il faiſoit auſſi clair comme de iour, paſſerent par deſſus le pont-neuf, entre 8. & 9. heures du ſoir, Samedi 13. il fut poſé dans l'Ancienne Egliſe du College Diuin de ce grand perſonnage Iean Sorbonne, dont il eſt Imitateur & Reſtaurateur d'icelle Maiſon & d'vne Magnifique Egliſe qu'il a fait baſtir à la gloire de Dieu, lieu deſtiné pour l'inhumer.

A PARIS, Par François Beauplet, Libraire & Imprimeur, en l'Iſle du Palais, au Signe de la Croix. 1642.

Index

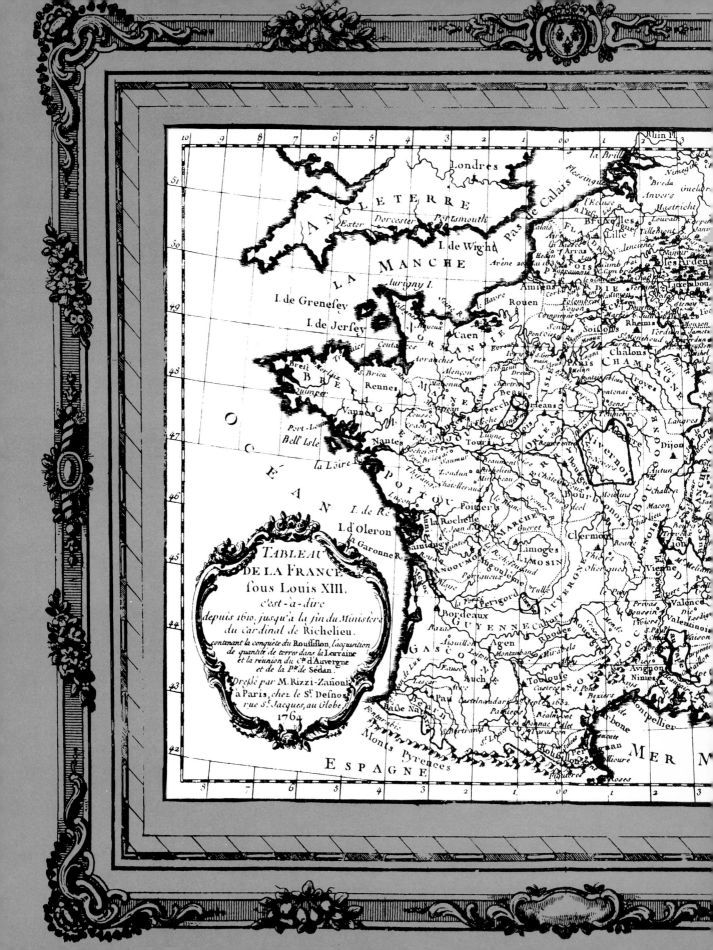

GREY EMINENCE, by Jean
Léon Gérôme. A typical nineteenth-century academic version
of the legend of Richelieu and
Père Joseph. The latter is seen
in solitary study before a tapestry
of the Cardinal's crest while visiting courtiers fawn. (Courtesy
Museum of Fine Arts, Boston.)